T0268903

THE TECHNOLOGY OF INTENTION

THE TECHNOLOGY OF INTENTION

Activating the Power of the Universe within YOU!

KIM STANWOOD TERRANOVA

 DEVORSS PUBLICATIONS
CAMARILLO, CA

THE TECHNOLOGY OF INTENTION
Copyright © 2020
by Kim Stanwood Terranova

PRINT ISBN: 9780875169040
EBOOK ISBN: 9780875169057

Third Printing, 2024

DeVorss & Company, Publisher
P.O. Box 1389
Camarillo CA 93011-1389
www.devorss.com

Printed in the United States of America

Library of Congress Cataloging-in-Publication Data
    Names: Terranova, Kim Stanwood, author.
    Title: The technology of intention : activating the power of the universe within you / Kim Stanwood Terranova.
    Description: First Edition. | Camarillo : DeVorss Publications, 2020. |
    Identifiers: LCCN 2019041834 (print) | LCCN 2019041835 (ebook) |
    ISBN 9780875169040 (trade paperback) | ISBN 9780875169057 (ebook)
    Subjects: LCSH: Intentionalism. | Self-actualization (Psychology)
    Classification: LCC BF619.5 .T47 2020 (print) | LCC BF619.5 (ebook) | DDC
       158.1--dc23
    LC record available at https://lccn.loc.gov/2019041834
    LC ebook record available at https://lccn.loc.gov/2019041835

Table of Contents

Acknowledgments

Acknowledgments are among my favorite things. The power to truly see someone rightly, to honor them, to be grateful for them, it is such an important blessing. So, at this moment, I am aware of how many beautiful souls I wish to thank, those souls that walked with me on this journey to complete this book. There were countless individuals, so many I am so very grateful for.

Without the inspiration and endless support of my teacher and mentor Michael Bernard Beckwith, this book would not be possible, my life would not be the adventure it is. He has walked with me for countless years, inspiring me, guiding me and always, always, holding me to the light and seeing the truth for me even when I could not see it myself. I thank him from the overflow of my heart. I asked him once, "How can I ever thank you enough?" He answered, "You already have, your life is a thank-you."

My beautiful practitioner Rev. Kathleen McNamara has held me in her powerful prayers, and always known the truth for me when I may have forgotten it. I thank her with all my heart, I love her with all my soul.

My two precious children, Lucas and Lila. They have put up with me asking them daily, "What is your intention?" and they never threw anything at me! They each continued to stay engaged in the process of our individual and collective expansion. They are my inspiration and my life and my greatest teachers of love. My heart expands in appreciation of them, as they said yes to walk this lifetime with me.

I am forever grateful to the two greatest parents, David and Peggy Stanwood. They continue to stand next to me while I grow, and lift me up when I fall. Their love created the space for me to embark upon writing this book, they told me I could do anything, and I believed them. Thank you to my brother David, for his love and acceptance of all my endeavors.

My publisher, Gary Peattie, said yes to me and has honored my vision in a way that is life changing. My appreciation to him is all consuming, and his trust in me is a blessing beyond measure. I thank DeVorss Publications for trusting me and saying YES to this diving partnership of fulfilled intention! Then, of course, my magnificent editor Mary Miller. Her gentleness combined with strength and articulate writing capacity kept my creation alive and clear. I am honored to have her touch the pages with her wisdom and grace.

It is an understatement to say I have exquisite friends, as I truly am surrounded by the most exceptional people. Denise Martinez Joyce, thank you for believing in me and being my biggest fan, I am eternally grateful to you. Although your vision of my gifts took me a while to step into, you consistently and lovingly held the light upon the path so I could see the way! Michelle McCarthy, you stood for me, you stand for me, you guide me and inspire me daily, I love you and thank you. Eric Davis, without you, I am not complete. We have lived our lives together, grown together and you always push me onward to complete everything I came here to deliver. Thank you! Lydia and Bill Beetley, thank you for gifting me your beautiful space to relax into as I surrendered to write for days. Words can never thank you enough for your unending love, friendship and support to myself and my children. My heart is filled with gratitude to you! Michelle Jackson, you feed my soul, and our adventures in life have changed my life. Thank you my friend! Pam Oslie, your guidance, deep friendship and unlimited capacity saw my expansion before I could. I love you for so much! Lori and Carey Hayes, for over twenty years you two have assisted me with living my dreams, and I would not wish to experience this life without YOU. Thank God I never have to!

Kimberly Gamble, your belief in me, your inspiration in this work and your insistence that my job was to complete this work, I can never thank you enough. Rhonda Britten, you pointed me in the direction of leading an intentional life, and your wisdom and aim for excellence has continued to uplift me and inspire me. Harley Jane Kozak, you are a treasure and I thank you for being a treasure of a friend! Alison Pacheco, your love and deep friendship illuminates me and infuses me with laughter. Victoria Freeman, I thank you for your faith in me, and for the most delicious brownies that kept me awake and present to keep going. Ginette Lemonnier, thank you for clearing the glass for me to see more accurately through. My PVHS girlfriends, thank you for a lifetime of laughter, and for loving me even when I could not be there at times, as I was deep in the pages of what was being created.

The two Lindas, wonderful Rev. Linda Fisher and magnificent Linda Ruoho, thank you for walking with me, lifting me, supporting my expansion and always loving me. Linda Ruoho, your guidance, divine articulation, perfect edits of every revision and brilliance in assisting me in all ways is a blessing beyond measure, and I thank you forever! Paola Castro, thank you for creating the space for this cover photo to be birthed! I am eternally grateful we found our way to each other in this lifetime! Nicole Rager, thank you for asking me the best question at the perfect moment to create a divine connection for this book to be manifested! Lucinda Bassett, I so appreciate your outlining input to complete this book and get it to the world! My fabulous photographer, Javier Mereb — his willingness to see the vision I was aiming to articulate, and then creating it. I am so grateful to him! Thank you to beautiful Costa Rica, the sands and ocean that inspired this cover creation!

It is so important to mention. My clients, they inspire me each and every day. They have been willing to trust me, to put into practice these principles and to keep on when the keeping on was hard. I honor each of them and I am so beyond blessed that they are in my life. A very special mention to Ashley and Camryn Cunningham, who said yes to living a life of intention for over ten years now, and they are evidence of manifestations amplified as they continue to embody a life of bold spiritual practice.

To all those challenges that came my way, every one of them, thank you for making me stronger to climb every mountain and more determined to reach my dreams.

May I not forget my sweetest Juliet and Brando, my four-legged loves that kept the kisses in overflow to keep me writing. I owe this book to them too!

Dedication

This book is dedicated to the four glorious light beams that illuminate my heart and are my world, my parents David and Peggy Stanwood, and my precious children, Lucas and Lila. I love you all to the moon and back and around the Universe a million times!

Foreword

BY MICHAEL BERNARD BECKWITH

OVER THE YEARS, people have heard me teach that most people suffer from an "intentional deficit disorder." Lives kind of meander as individuals are captivated by the emotional contagion of the day, whatever happens to be trending, or are pulled by their perception of past experiences. Intention, as a spiritual faculty and practice, radically shifts us to an authentic, meaningful life lived on purpose.

The Technology of Intention is a wonderful, important and timely book for the planet right now. Not only is the information it contains transformative, it provides a greater understanding of intentionality itself. Kim Stanwood Terranova beautifully shows you the art and the science of its practice. If you have been drifting in your life, this is the book for you.

My relationship with Kim has spanned decades. She first rode into Agape International on her motorcycle every

Sunday morning, and now as a licensed spiritual therapist, she graces the stage of Agape as one of my teachers and speakers. Not only have I trusted Kim with teaching the core tenets from my own books *Spiritual Liberation* and *The Answer Is You*, I have also witnessed the depth and profundity of her own teachings. We have traveled together, walked a spiritual path together, and she has grown into a leader of transformational wisdom. Her life is a powerful testament to what it means to live with intention.

I have watched Kim live an intentional life when things were going magnificently for her, and I have also seen how she copes with tremendous challenges. I witnessed her gracefully release a long-term marriage. More recently, I observed the resilient way she set about rebuilding her home after it was burned by the Malibu fires in 2018.

Kim is the real deal.

She is a powerful teacher and speaker who leaves her audiences with a sense of unlimited possibility and empowered inspiration. She delivers the goods, the tools to live a life of spiritual awakening and expansive healing. Her intention is to assist all individuals she walks with to break free of any self-imposed boundaries, and to create a life of illumination, pure joy, and as the untethered self-expression of Spirit's vision for their lives.

This book, *The Technology of Intention*, teaches you that instead of being influenced by external circumstances, you can take charge of your life. You will be surprised how living an intentional life will bring about blessings and gifts that are way bigger than what you may have dared to imagine for yourself.

Intention is the key to life. Living in intention means co-creating your life as a result of your everyday choices. Without intention, life happens *to* us, not *through* us.

We came into the world with everything we need to fulfill our destiny. Intention is the way to uncover our inherent giftedness. Adding clear intentions as a means of supporting our focused desire amplifies the field of consciousness, bringing all that we desire to us with grace and ease.

Perhaps you are someone who has great expectations for your life. Kim shows you that expectation isn't enough. She shows you why it's fundamentally different from participating in creating our dream. When we are in expectation, it takes us out of a creative mode. We expect something to happen outside of ourselves, whereas the trick is to *envision and create* it from within.

Clarity is powerful. If we wish to create all that we desire, we must be really clear what we are asking for. The powerful infusion of crystal clarity creates unbridled energy that can bring forth an unparalleled manifestation. Call forth what you wish for, and simultaneously release what you do not wish to experience. You can do this by getting in the habit of choosing words that empower, uplift and convey a positive vibration. Positive words that address the present moment in a proactive way are life-changing.

This book will help you embrace the faculty of your *attention*, which will give you a greater level of dominion over it. This will allow you to unleash your underlying intention for everything your life has the potential to be.

Kim not only gives you a greater understanding of intentionality, she also shares sacred practices that will enable you to become adept at participating in your own glorious unfoldment. I know that she wants for you a life beyond what society offers you—a life that transcends anything you may ever have dreamed of for yourself. Accept her invitation.

Michael Bernard Beckwith
Founder & Spiritual Director, Agape International Spiritual Center
Author, *Life Visioning and Spiritual Liberation*

Introduction

THERE IS NO DOUBT that our world is fueled by the power of technology and that we have before us the opportunity to utilize this power on a daily basis. Technology has blessed our lives and made it possible for us to know what is happening on the other side of the world within seconds. We have the ability to access information, to communicate around the world, to build businesses, to market material, co-create projects and reach millions of people, all through the use of technology. Our computers and phones have become appendages and there are times we feel as if we are missing something if we have not regularly checked in on social media or the information highway. Often in a crowded social space one will see masses of humans with their faces looking down at a screen, all eyes on the power of technology at their fingertips. Life has changed! The connection of the divine, of looking into the eyes of another, has shifted; instead, we look at a screen.

At this time in human history, it is more important than ever for us to remember that we each have within us our own inner technology, and it is calling us. Our inner sanctuary of divine wisdom is our intimate point of unlimited guidance, and if we ignore it, we shall be an out-of-balance society. Looking into screens for answers instead of looking into our souls. The key is balance! We can choose to appreciate technology and utilize it for all the blessings it gives us, while simultaneously cultivating our soul's calling as we remember the power within. The merging, the dance of honoring the inner wisdom within each of us while activating the information highway through the use of technology is mind-boggling to think of all that can be created. It is not one or the other, it is the merging of both! To live a life of balance in the world today, we must cultivate and nurture our spiritual wisdom with as much focus as we use to keep up with the speed of technology.

To illuminate the power of this inner technology, we must be awake. This book is about being awake, really awake, and staying alert to our choices while remembering the ability we each have to choose to access this power within, to tap into our own inner technology. It has been proven that everything is energy, and we are the energetic beings that have choice at our fingertips. The activation point is us, and the Universe is awaiting our consistent practice to honor all we have within our DNA and create from that connection! We build our lives choice by choice, moment by moment, and sometimes we are not staying conscious of what we are creating. Then we wonder why something occurred that we did not see coming. Staying conscious is a priority and we are hardwired with an inner technology that awaits our willingness, our belief and our readiness to stay awake, present and conscious!

Words have power. We can create or destroy with the language we choose to use. We are bodies of energy moving in this time continuum together and technology of intention propels action into motion as we activate the energy of the Universe by the power of our words.

Intentions give us the pathway to consciously create our lives. They are the powerful force that points the energy in the direction of all we wish to manifest. This book is a map and a guiding light in assisting us to not only understand the power we each have, but to also give us the road map and step-by-step process to ignite that power. We all have the ability to co-create our lives, and the use of intentions make it possible. The pages before you will guide you to embrace the adventure of living a life of loving response to yourself and others. A life created by choice, a life that impacts the world because you choose to be conscious of your imprint upon the world. Your choice, your intention opens the door to unstoppable and unlimited blessings. We are all in this together, we are all here to wake up together and create a world that honors all beings!

For over two decades I have worked with clients, assisting them to live a life of powerful intention. The experiences that I have observed as they chose to build an ongoing practice of creating by intention is beyond incredible. Individuals have shifted their relationships, increased their business, doubled and tripled their financial success, healed their bodies, enhanced their family relationships and so much more. These individuals did not know "how" to do this when they began but they had one thing in common: they were willing to be willing! They practiced even when they were not sure how their dreams would manifest. They were committed to aiming their compass toward their desires with clarity, power and, most importantly, faith. They trusted that somehow their words would be heard, their prayers would be answered, and they were! All of them reaped the rewards of a life of expansive joy and success and they continue to keep reaping unlimited success in all that they aim for. There is no stopping once you experience a life of full-throttle manifestation!

The beautiful thing is that this power is at your fingertips, or better yet, at the tip of your consciousness. It has always been there, awaiting your activation. You have always had it, even as you took your first breath. It has never left you, and it never will, yet only you can tap into it. You hold the key to your destiny within your soul. Breath by breath, word by word, action by action, your destiny lies within your power. You are the creative force that lights up the path of fulfillment. The power to experiencing your greatest desires lies within your willing heart. You can choose right here, right now, to say YES on a grand level. It's a yes that will change the life you have known, a yes that will expand your paradigm and lift you to new heights! YOU are the yes. So, I ask you, are you willing?

THE TECHNOLOGY OF INTENTION

CHAPTER 1

The Power Is Within YOU

You hold the power to your destiny at the
touch of your fingertips; it is your very breath.

CONGRATULATIONS! You have just taken the first
step toward transforming your life and opening yourself up
to unlimited possibilities in every area of your beautiful existence. Now, get ready, your entire life as you have known it
is about to change. There is no way it cannot! You will be a
different person after applying the tools of living an intentional life, and that is a beautiful thing. Why would anyone want
to be the same next year, next week? We have done that, been
there, no need to repeat the past. It is time for something fresh
and new. It is time for transformational living!

I believe we all desire to live a life of unlimited joy, deep
peace and abundant happiness, yet we may not know the

direction to take, or we may not feel we have the tools needed to fulfill that desire. The greatest teachers have taught us that there is a path, a key to living in expansive happiness and peace. That magical key is the knowingness that the path always begins within. The journey home, the adventure of going within is the path to unlimited freedom and joy. All signs throughout history, time after time, direct us to the exploration of the inner world of self discovery. The inner chambers of our soul hold the pearl of deep wisdom.

It may be a journey that takes courage to explore, yet it is a process of discovery that will change our life. The path is at our beck and call, and we can choose to take the adventure to walk, skip or fly down the path, or we can choose to sit it out! It is always our choice.

As we observe all the blessings for which scientific technology has shifted and impacted our lives dramatically, it is imperative to simultaneously acknowledge that there is also a spiritual technology in place. This spiritual technology is something that each of us has access to, and it is our birthright to activate it at any given moment we choose. When I speak of spiritual technology, I am referring to the tools that support us and empower us to live in conscious contact with Spirit, the Universe or God, whatever we name it. The tools that awaken our soul and mind, the tools that keep us present and available for more good than we can imagine. They include and expand beyond meditation, prayer, visioning, gratitude, acknowledgment, transformational breath-work, visualization, yoga and my personal favorite, INTENTION! The power of the conscious use of intention propels action into being. YOU have the power to activate intention to create all you desire! You have this spiritual technology, the technology of intention at your beck and call, and you now get to embody it! Living in intention is co-creating your life by choice and power. Intention-setting moves mountains and creates miracles because we are at one with the power of the unlimited nature of the Universe. Without intention, life happens to us, not through us. Intentions are clear statements that are based in the qualities of all you wish to experience and are propelled into motion by you! They keep you out of expectation, disappointment and searching for circumstantial evidence to be happy. Amplified intentional living brings you unbounded happiness and fulfillment!

My own self discovery is what awakened me to the magnificent truth that we do actually create our lives from the inside out, and that we have the tools for the journey already programmed within us. We came with all we need to fulfill our destiny in this lifetime, but we must have the willingness to live in steadfast curiosity to apply what we begin to discover and uncover! The acceptance that there is more than we may see with our human eye is the key to keeping us curious, courageous, alive and engaged! If we are willing to stay in the game of life, to want to live full out and activate the ability to create consciously, we can experience unbounded joy and profound fulfillment. This book is about actualizing, embodying and having a direct experience of remembering who you are and living in the full truth that you can create all you wish for!

MY SEARCH

I think it is important to get a glimpse of how this book came to be, or how the beginning came to be, I should say. The story or pieces of it will unfold within these pages, yet I feel it is important to understand the journey of its creation.

I always wanted to understand more about the workings of the world, but it was not until I was 22 that I began searching in earnest.

I felt very alone in my search and I desperately wanted clarity on how to live a fulfilled life, how to truly know what I wanted to be, do, have and how to achieve it. I wanted to know why I was here, what it all was for and why I had this aching inner urge to uncover the Truth, whatever that I set out to discover answers. Let me be clear, at this point it was not by joy that I set out, it was by desperation. I was hurting and wanted answers to the confusion I was living in. Many years later in my life, I learned from a very powerful teacher of mine that, "You are either pushed by the pain or pulled by the vision." At that point in my life, it was very clear that I fell under the first category, of being pushed by the pain. The sadness and ache in my heart was from not understanding what life was about. But this sadness and desperation led to powerful action. I became unstoppable in my hunt.

I read every book I could get my hands on, anything that could guide me to understand the power of what we could create, and how to activate the energy of the Universe. I drove my family and friends crazy (I have been told), as I was relentless. I would give them a book, they would hand it back to me the next day and say they just didn't get it and they were not sure what I was up to. I wanted to have deep conversations with everyone. What was the use of small talk? Then one day, while walking into a modeling job I was hired to do in San Francisco, I met someone who finally understood. Spirit had blessed me with a soul who would become very impactful on my journey. This beautiful angel was hired for the same job, so the two of us had four days together. I'm not sure how well we did posing next to the product for those four days (as we were hired to do), but I do know I was being fed information that I had been starving for as long as I could remember. Information I had been asking the Universe for. I was ecstatic!

The next weekend this beautiful woman named Rhonda invited me to meet her and her husband at a spiritual center in the Oakland Hills of California. She told me this is where she had been studying, and said I might be interested. I had only dabbled in church growing up, my family did not regularly attend anywhere and my participation at church occurred on Christmas Eve or following a friend after a sleepover to their place of worship on Sunday morning. I did not realize that this experience on this certain Sunday morning was not going to be anything like I had ever experienced. I walked into a beautiful space with an adorable petite powerful redheaded minister that was soon to be one of the answers to the next step upon my journey. She was going to point me in the direction of deep and profound healing.

Here is what I know now happened that Sunday morning when I was 22. I was awakened, and questions I had held onto for years were starting to get answered. I was told that the power of the Universe is within me and I did not have to search outside myself to understand who I was. I learned that I had direct contact with this power, whether one calls it God, Source, Spirit or the Universe, and I learned that it was all love. This energetic force moves through me, and it and I are one. I learned that there was no separation from source energy and myself and I had direct access to the unlimited nature of the Universe.

I cried.

I cried some more.

And then I cried some more. Thank goodness this "church" had tissues close by!

My life was changed that day. Wonderful Rev. Margaret Stortz, in the Oakland Church of Religious Science, had just awakened me to the fact that nothing was wrong with me.

I may have been "odd" in my fanatical search, but at least there were other odd ones out there that I could now relate to! I was beyond elated!

So, my journey into the depths of spiritual study, new thought ageless wisdom, metaphysical knowledge and so much more began. The floodgates had opened and I was never turning back. Full throttle ahead was my motion! All I was interested in was how to learn more as fast as possible. The fire in me had been ignited. I just turned the corner from being pushed by the pain to being propelled by the vision!

> *The secret of harmonious living is the development of spiritual consciousness.*
>
> Joel S. Goldsmith

Developing my spiritual consciousness became my life. Deepening my connection to Spirit was my commitment from that moment onward. Understanding that the gift was at hand and the power within was tangible changed everything. I know without a shadow of a doubt that the most potent form of energy is thought. From that blessed day in that sacred space in the Oakland Hills, and each day since, I am more clear and conscious of the truth that we are what we think about and we create from our thoughts. The power and presence of the Universe is unlimited by its very nature, and it resides within us! There is no separation from this source energy that some of us call God, or Spirit or the Universe. It is all ONE! And we are one with it. So, the unlimited power resides within us, we have access to the most potent energy, thought, and we can create anything we desire! OMGoodness! Absolutely miraculous!

Each and every one of us has full access. Each and every one of us deserves to live an unlimited life. All limitation resides within our thinking, and we all have the power to remove it. It is just a belief and we have the tools to remember who we are and release the beliefs that no longer serve us. It may take practice, and it may take willingness, and it will definitely take an open heart, but it is more than possible. It is *probable* that our intentions will manifest. Once you begin to choose to embody the tools presented on the pages of this book, all of your life will begin to unfold in spectacular ways!

One of the most beautiful things about this thing called life is that the Universe has left us signs along the path that assist us in remembering who we are. Just as in the fairy tales of our childhood, there are always signs for us to follow if only we stay open and aware to receive them. To live in this human existence and to live a spiritually awakened life, it is necessary to remember who we are and to follow the signs that Spirit is blessing us with.

Remember who you are!

Mufasa, Lion King

The pathway to remembering begins with a willingness to cultivate the connection to the Universal Presence. Staying in conscious contact with Spirit is of the utmost importance when we are aiming to live in our Oneness and consciously create our lives. This energetic force is guiding us every moment. The more we muddle up our thoughts, the harder it is to stay conscious of the direct contact to Spirit. So, it is vitally important to keep the channel clear to stay connected to this powerful energy.

When we are connected, we are open to deep listening, which ultimately keeps us available to being given information and being guided. This powerful field is sourcing us with all we need at any given time. So, as we keep the connection clear, we are tapping into the energetic field and receiving what we need with each step we take. It is our very breath! This is where the importance of our practice comes to play. One's willingness to practice is everything.

When we are keeping our daily practice in place, then our availability to stay in conscious contact is much more tangible. It becomes everything! Our job is to keep the channel to Spirit clear so there is no interruption of conscious contact. The signs along the path are seen with eyes wide open when we are keeping our minds and hearts available to the direction of source energy. Once you begin cultivating this field of awareness and stay awake to this loving presence in your life, you will never be the same. It only gets richer and deeper with each breath you take. And if you already have a strong conscious connection with Spirit, then acknowledge yourself and let's now begin to dive deeper into all that is possible for you in evolving to the next paradigm of your own inner expansion!

> *Whatever we believe comes true for us.*
>
> Louise L. Hay

All of this comes back to knowing that the power of creation lives within us and we need not search endlessly to find it. It is imperative that we seek out the teachers and tools that assist us in remembering who we are, that ignite our inner knowing. Walking the path, however, is our charge. We can learn, read and study, but ultimately, we are the decision makers, choosing to take a breath, to move onward despite conditions and to practice even when it is dark. We have the tools. We were encoded with them as we came into this lifetime. It is all about the path of remembering!

You have the opportunity to awaken and remember. You hold the key. May you be free in knowing that the journey you have been upon has brought you right here to be willing to expand to the next level of your evolution. Let us begin together to create from a conscious high choice awareness!

Remember to remember!

Let us choose to embody a life of intention so that we are creating from a desire to experience what we want, versus unconsciously expecting things to just happen for us. When we are activating high intentions, when we are implementing an intentional life, using the tool of INTEN-TION, then we are creating with the unlimited power of all that is. Intentions give direction to our desires so the Universe can assist us in creating them! Simple as that! Without intention, one tends to get stuck in unconscious expectation, which leads to a life of disappointment. We have the key at our fingertips!

My deepest wish for you is that you have the tools and the willingness to live in the vibration of unlimited possibility and co-create your life in the manner you so desire! It is my intention to offer you the tools I have found and assist you in creating ways to stay conscious upon your journey. Let us embark upon this adventure together to illuminate pathways for you to experience all that your heart wishes for. If you are here reading these words, then you have been directed by your soul to grow. Please know that I am honored to be with you on the path of your personal and unique unfoldment. Now let's get busy!

 **REMEMBER**

With each breath, the
power is within YOU!

CHAPTER 2

The Big I, Intention

Intention lines up with the unlimited source
of the Universe and manifests through YOU!

THE UNIVERSE is just waiting for our clear intention so it can assist us in the creation of all we desire! All activation of full-throttle manifestation comes through the power of intention. Simple as that. Spiritual wisdom, spiritual technology, at its finest. Technology is speeding up everywhere in the world, changing our world and our lives faster than we can blink. The blessings of it are palpable. It is necessary to stay alert and in balance during such massive progress, and this is only done by keeping our spiritual practices as close as our breath!

It is of vital importance, as if our lives depended on it, because they do. If we miss this ever-important detail we

will become a society that is off-center, one-sided and completely detached from our inner power and connection to
one another. The technology in spirituality is the pathway
to keep us balanced! This technology is some of the most
important technology of your life, because you are the creator of your life.

My aim is to assist YOU to stay alert and present to
activating this unlimited power of technology within you,
so you have the keys to the kingdom at your fingertips. The
keys have always been within you, the ability to manifest
with ease. You just forgot the pathway. It is time to remember, it is time to stay alert, awake and empowered to create
all that you dream of. This is the most important thing, to
stay awake, and create consciously, for the good of ourselves
and everyone else we are walking with.

Staying awake serves you and serves humanity . . . the
world is hungry for us to live an awakened life!

Our world is moving so fast due to the blessings of technology, and if we do not embody our spiritual technology at
the same speed, then we will be an out-of-balance society.

Intention is power!

Intention creates!

You are the access point!

The power to create whatever you wish is within you, and the access point is learning to embody clear and concise intentions. The BIG I is the activating force that propels miracles into being. The BIG I is descriptive of my favorite word, INTENTION! Ask anyone, they will tell you, my most asked question to all far and near, and at any given moment, is, "What is your intention?" So, I am now asking you,

"What is YOUR intention?"

Think about it, because your answer can change your life. Your intention will change your life, so it is worth truly understanding the depth of living a life of powerful intention.

The core of spiritual technology resides in utilizing this practice of cultivating clear intentions in our life. The power is at our fingertips, or even more accurately, at the point of our very breath. With every inhale and every exhale, we can choose to be alert to what we are intending. The unlimited field is awaiting our direction, so it is of utmost importance that we be awake to what we aim for! The pathway that leads to divine fulfillment is the wisdom to walk not only understanding the depth of intention but to truly live it. To learn it and live it is power, and how good it is to know that each of us has our own magic wand filled with unlimited power right within us.

I believe there is a huge difference between knowledge and wisdom. Someone can have lots of knowledge, they can know something front and back and all around, but if they are not living it, embodying it, then it is just information. It may be good information, but it is stagnated if it is not being lived and fully embodied.

Knowledge unused or not accessed does not change the world or change lives. It is like a magnificent library filled with gorgeous and important books. If the books in the library are never read, and their knowledge not applied or embodied, then that library is just a beautiful location to house pretty things. Some of us are very pretty beings, with a mind full of information, but we are not activating our potential and power if we are not living what we know. The key is, we must live the knowledge we have. We must be willing to activate it, practice it and learn more.

That is the difference between knowledge and wisdom: one is information, the other is living the information. It is an intention of mine to embody wisdom and to apply the knowledge I have learned and continue to learn so that my presence can make a difference in this world. It is also my intention to assist you to live a life of wisdom by applying the knowledge that you have! To truly live what you know! And the path to do that is by amplifying the technology of intention.

My client, Ashley, completely altered the direction of her life the moment she began to utilize this technology — not just by hearing me talk about it week after week or by listening to my repetitive question of "What is your intention in this situation?" Her life changed the minute SHE became willing to begin to live her life by intention. That was her access point to fulfillment.

Why did you not tell me that once I began living a life of intention, my entire life would change for the better? . . . Oh yeah, you did tell me, and I finally just began doing it, and nothing will ever be the same!

My Client, Ashley

Although Ashley had been on the path in our one-on-one sessions for some time, the determining moment came when she decided to utilize this tool. Instantly her relationships shifted to a higher vibration, she had a sense of calm knowing, and she suddenly truly understood that whatever confronted her in life, she would be able to move through it. She tapped into the unlimited source! It was life-changing. Her experiences in life altered dramatically and she was no longer living with any expectation of how things should work out, or disappointed that they were not working out as she wanted! She began dropping all expectation and standing present in creating consciously with every intention she uttered. And her life has never been the same!

I have watched thousands of people change their lives by applying this technology and living a life of powerful intention. The same can happen for you! Simply put, our intentions manifest with accuracy when we are attentive in how we create them. In the pages that follow I will teach YOU how to create clear and powerful intentions so that you are experiencing all that you desire. Your willingness to grow, to apply your heart-based knowledge is all that is necessary for the journey. The willingness to be present to writing focused intentions is your point of transformation. The power of creating life consciously is the activation point of intention. It is that easy!

It excites me to even think about what you are about to create. You see, this magnificent, beautiful force, energetic field, Spirit, the Universe, whatever you wish to call it, is awaiting your YES. It is just simply awaiting your yes, and your access. As you set your intentions, you are activating the field of unlimited possibility to create through you, and when this happens, all possibility exists at your beck and call. Did you catch that? ALL possibility exists at your beck and call! Ah, when we allow this knowledge to sink into our awareness, we begin to see how much responsibility we have in this lifetime. We are responsible to create the life we wish! And the power exists at the core of our intentions! This is GREAT news! You hold the power within you!

Intentions direct the action of your life.
Intentions create your life.
Intentions are your life!

WHAT EXACTLY ARE INTENTIONS?

Intentions are energetically lasered statements that inform the Universe of your desire and the direction in which you wish it to be fulfilled. Intentions are based on qualities of experiences and are always stated in the positive, present tense. They are the guiding light, the directing force in determining all that you manifest. Intentions are the through line to a good script. They lift us, they keep us focused, and they keep us awake and aware of where we are headed. Most importantly they keep us out of expectation and disappointment, and ground us in the present moment.

Intentions are the propelling energy of all action that is aimed to create the life you wish. Think about that: they are the driving force! Without them, it's as if you are driving blindfolded. Would you ever drive your car blindfolded? NO! So why would you live without being clear about your intentions?

An important thing to note is this: intentions are similar to what most of us know as goals, yet they are very uniquely different. Goals have a certain pre-determined outcome.

This is not bad, as goals are highly effective and magnificent, but they are different from what I am referring to here when I speak of intentions. Intentions have an aim, they are specific, yet they also are open to allow the Universe to infuse them with unlimited solutions and possibilities that we may not see with our human eye. They are also different to the extent that intentions tend to have more momentum to them and usually are not as rigid as goals. Remember this, they are both powerful tools, and the intention setting we are discussing here has a potency of power from the unlimited realms of consciousness, so they manifest bigger and more vibrant than the human-imposed limitations of goals.

A simple, starter intention looks like this:

My intention is to stay conscious and kind in all
conversations today and connect with all those
I come in contact with!

The above example is a lasered statement that is clear, in the present moment and based in a quality of life. The sentence is stating to the Universe that you are aiming to be kind and conscious with others. If you have an intention such as this, to connect with all those you come into contact with, you will be much more likely to show up present in your conversations. Your communication skills will be propelled by kindness. All conversations change dramatically when we show up being present and kind. Without an aim, you may show up in interactions a bit distracted, not fully present, your mind on other things and not completely aware and conscious of the words you are using while talking to someone. This is what happens when we are not creating consciously. Then we wonder why we are not having relationships or experiences in life that are authentic. The power is in our ability and choice to create with awareness and intentional focus. And this is just the beginning!

Here are the facts: we are creative beings and we are always creating either consciously or unconsciously. When we are unconscious in our creation, then we are creating by default. Thoughts run through our mind every second. Unconscious thoughts can cause havoc if they are thoughts of fear, uncertainty, lack, anger or judgment. It is evident that the challenge comes when we are creating unconsciously, or by default, as then we are often creating a lot of things we do not want. And we do not even know we are doing it!

When we are unaware, it is as if we are a ship with no direction in a vast and expansive sea, just floating aimlessly. The ship may crash into rocks, or the shore, or possibly keep floating, but without any desired destination. When you choose to set your intention each day, you are aiming your ship, guiding your thinking process in the direction of all that you desire.

You are not just allowing your thoughts to run amuck to bring back experiences that you truly may not want. I invite you to be the captain of your ship, to stay alert to all that you are creating and to activate this inner power with focus so that it brings all that you dream of to you.

Living a life of intention guarantees you will not be floating aimlessly without direction, but rather directed with strength and focus. This practice of creating conscious intentions is beyond life altering. Everything will change in your life when you begin to incorporate intentions on a regular basis. Let me say that again to make sure you really hear me:

Everything will change in your life when you begin to incorporate intentions on a regular basis.

We gain momentum with each intention we set, with each time we focus our energy on our intentions. The Universe is awaiting your clear intention to bring forth all you wish to experience. Clarity is power, and the clearer your intentions are, the more likely it is they will come rushing back to you in great measure with accuracy and speed. The truth is that you can shift your life into great manifestation if you work with your intentions. It is said in AA that it works if you keep working it. The twelve-step program has saved the lives of millions of people, and they have it right: it works if you keep working it.

Transformation requires that our attention align with our intention.

When attention and intention conjoin, a powerful vortex of awareness is generated that keeps us mindful and in the "now" moment!

Michael Bernard Beckwith

The bottom line is, what you focus on expands, and when you focus on thoughts of abundance, joy, happiness, fulfillment, divine relationships and such, then that is what expands in your life and ultimately what you experience. Adding clear intentions to support your focused desire only amplifies the field of consciousness to bring all that you desire to you with grace and ease. You are focusing on all that you desire, and that is what will come to you.

We gain momentum in life when we are clear and strong. The same with intentions. The more clarity we use when creating them, the stronger the outcome will be. We have the ability to honor the gift of language and choose to be clear with the words we use when we create our intentions. The power of our words is potent, and the choice we make in how to use our words is the key to joy-filled creation.

Language is a beautiful art and many of us do not realize how important it is to stay alert to what words we are using on a regular basis. Every word has energy, and when we add emotion to fuel the energy of our words, then the language we use propels movement. It is imperative that we stay alert to the words we choose to use as we move through our lives. Words have power! Consider the vibration of these sentences:

I never do anything right.

Nothing ever works out for me.

I am the black sheep in my family.

I am not smart enough.

I am too old to do that now.

My life is a mess.

Feel the vibration of how those words land on your heart, and if they give you energy or take energy from you. Do you feel empowered by them? Do they lift you or bring your energy down? Notice and observe!

Now consider these possible sentences:

I am open to grow in this situation.

All things, even the seeming challenges,
keep unfolding for my good.

Life is a miracle.

I am grateful for this moment, for the
ability to breathe.

I choose to be kind to myself today.

I invite you to repeat these sentences a few times and check yourself to see how you feel. Where did these sentences land in your heart? Notice I did not say land in your *head*. I am inviting you to see where they land in your heart! Listen and feel with your heart, as language is powerful and it lands in our emotional field.

What this leads to is an awareness of how much power we have in choosing what words we activate. By staying present to words that uplift, we create intentions that are in alignment with what we wish to experience, and the vibration of the language is propelled into motion. The language of our intentions is very important indeed! Language has power and you get to choose how to use that power.

Your actions follow your intentions.

Your feelings are the fuel that drive your intentions.

Use this book as a daily guide and you will experience a shift in your life. Now, this requires practice. It requires a willingness to practice. If you look at these intentions once and not again, your creation will not shift in dramatic ways. If you choose to work these words, to incorporate them into your daily practice, create them as part of your ongoing plan, then your life will most definitely change.

Maintaining an intention practice keeps you conscious, in the present moment and alert to creating all that you desire. I invite you to keep this book close to you and each day discover an intention for what supports you best at that moment. When you discover that intention, then read it, read it again, and see how it feels for you. If it is one that I have offered you here in this book, and you wish to alter a word or two to make it your own, do so.

The journey is about flexibility and living in divine flow. Just allow the words to flow through your conscious mind into your heart. Let them rest in your heart. Accept that this day, for this one day, you shall live by these words. During the day if you can refer back to your intention, that's even better. As often as possible go to the words and let them continue to sink into deeper levels of your consciousness. They can be your safe place to keep coming back to moment by moment. This is how you shift your life.

Your power resides at your point of connection with the divine presence within you. The Universal field awaits your willingness to connect and create unlimited possibilities. By boldly setting intentions, you are tapping into the unlimited power of the Universe!

Intentions are the driving force behind the full-throttle manifestation of your life as you desire. If you are prepared for your life to go into expansive creation, just get started on living an intentional life and nothing will stop the flow of goodness and abundance . . . NOTHING will stop the Universal Presence from delivering your good! It is just the way it works, and that is a good thing!

∾ REMEMBER ∾

Take a breath, set your intention and create. Stand tall with an open heart, live an intentional life, connect to the Universe and accept that all you desire is rushing toward you in this moment and always.
Intentions are Power!

CHAPTER 3

Intention Vs. Expectation

Releasing Expectations

EXPECTATION IS A TRICKY THING, and it seems to be a very human experience for many of us. The patterning to live in unconscious expectation can be found everywhere and appears to be widely accepted around the world. Most often the practice occurs in an unconscious state, but it occurs nonetheless. Expectation seeps into conversations, takes over in relationships and takes down friendships faster than you can blink. It sneaks in when we are not aware and conscious.

Often when humans are talking to one another, they do not even notice how often expectation has found its way into their conversation. It is very sneaky and conniving and can lead one down a path of great disappointment if there is no awareness that it is happening. When one is not creating his/her life consciously, then it is easy to unconsciously slip into living a life in expectation. And sadly, the expectation I am laying out here leads to a lot of heartache and disappointment.

Clarity is power and I want to be very clear about what I am stating here. The expectation I am referring to is this: any time you look for happiness and fulfillment to come from OUTSIDE of yourself, you will be disappointed. This might be hard to hear, so take a breath and let me try again.

When we are expecting things to be a certain way, people to behave in a specific manner, circumstances to be controlled in just the way we want them to be, we are in expectation. These are all outcomes that we cannot control. Yet over and over again, we try and try again, only to be disappointed. And this disappointment repeated over time eventually leads to symptoms of resentment, anger and frustration.

THE CHALLENGE

Very often we get stuck in the expectation itself, making it difficult for us to release. Again, remember I am referring to those expectations that are based outside of ourselves, not in the co-creating field. Many of them are based in unconscious patterning that we have either inherited or picked up along the way. When we do not even realize we are living in daily expectation, then the day-by-day disappointments come and we cannot figure out how to get through them.

There is a way out, but first we have to look at all the ways we allow ourselves to get caught up in expectation. Consider taking a look at something for a moment. I invite you to think back. Have you ever heard yourself saying anything similar to the following statements:

They should know how I like it to be done.

I cannot believe he/she has not texted me back yet.

My boss should know I deserve a raise by now.

My spouse must know I need that done.

If they just do this for me, I will be happy.

I give and give and never get anything back.

I would have been there on time but the traffic tripped me up.

The above statements and hundreds of others very similar to these are all signs of where we live in expectation. Our expectations lead us down the path of upset and consistent disappointment. The world we live in may have expectations everywhere, but it's our job as beings who wish to experience awake and conscious lives to see where the patterns of expectation exist and to do all we can to shift away from them. This takes practice, this takes gentleness, this takes high-conscious choice awareness. And all these things that it takes are present within you!

No matter how challenging it may seem in this moment, you have the power to release expectation and experience more happiness than you can imagine! Let us review what an expectation is defined as:

"A belief that I would or should achieve something."

When we do not even realize we are living in daily expectation, then the day-by-day disappointments multiply and we cannot figure out how to get through them. The challenge is, we are not usually even conscious of where they are coming from.

Expectations can be subtle (and usually are), quiet, sneaky and very draining. They keep our dreams out of reach because we unconsciously let expectation hold our attention and we are unaware it is happening. Our job is to get conscious and get conscious fast!

LET'S TALK ABOUT THE SHOULDS!

It's no mystery that the best friend of expectation is SHOULD, one of my least favorite words. Let me be more specific, I love words, and I love and appreciate language. I honor the potency and power of words and give them great value, so much so that I am very conscious of the words that roll off of my lips. I am also conscious of the words those around me use, and at times I admit that I hold people to their word more than they may be true to it. I have learned over the years to be watchful of my own use of words and flexible with others. I admit that it's been an important life lesson for me! Words have power; they are energy! How we use them is something to give attention to!

Now, I have been known to ask my clients if they would be willing to release the word "should" from their vocabulary. I bring it to their attention, as "should" has a certain weight to it. Listen to the word "should," hear how it rolls off your tongue and feel the energy behind it when you state it. I hear judgment in it and that is not something that I believe supports expansion and growth and deep connection. Judgment toward ourselves or others only leads to staying stuck or holding someone else hostage. One of my core intentions is to assist others in the evolution of their soul, of their own growth and expansion, so you can see why "should" is not a word that resonates well with me.

I don't see any empowering gifts to the word. It has expectation woven all through it. When we "should" ourselves, we are in judgment of ourselves. When we "should" others, we are in judgment of them. Typically, we are feeling disappointed that they did not fulfill our expectations of what we believe they "should" be doing or have done for us. Can you see the common theme here? So, I invite you to consider the same thing I propose to my clients. That is, blessing the word "should" and gently releasing it from your vocabulary for a while, and seeing how you feel. A powerful response or replacement word is "could." Shift a sentence like this:

"I should have done the job better; I did not do it very well at all."

"I could have done that a bit differently; I'll be more aware the next time."

Try it out for a bit and see how you feel. To those that may say "should" is necessary when criticizing a lack of responsibility, well, I suggest we consider what benefits judgment has in our lives. I would like to think if we utilized a little more discernment in situations, instead of judgment, then we may explore pathways to connect and resolve situations in a gentler manner. We have the opportunity to stay connected and kind instead of experiencing judgment and separation.

SOMETHING TO CONSIDER

Try it for a bit: simply replace your *should* with *could* and see how you feel. That is the best way to expand, so see how it fits for you!

Can you begin to see how our words have potency? The beautiful art of language has power, and how we choose to use our words can bring us a deep connection with ourselves and others, or create intense separation. It is our choice, always. Remember, if you intend that your day is going to turn out great, it most likely will. Yet, if you expect that your day will turn out great if a certain person does a certain thing for you, then you will be led to disappointment almost every time and feel resentful and frustrated. It's hard to experience the good when we are stuck in these emotions. It's challenging to stand in joyful creation when we are in the midst of heavy frustration because of what we thought would occur. When we live in expectation that our happiness is based on happenings outside of us, then we set ourselves up to be disappointed. How can we not? So, to have the ability to move from disappointment to joy and freedom is a powerful tool that can completely alter the direction of your life.

Now, take a breath, and somebody give me a drumroll: Here is the ticket *out* of living a life of expectation and disappointment.

Living a life of INTENTION keeps us out of EXPECTATION!

The ticket out is to begin creating clear intentions. It's as simple as that! Expectation can lead to disappointment, whereas intentions lead to freedom. We lose power in expectation, we gain power in intention. Disappointment follows expectation, intentions solve expectation.

We are aligning our power with the power of the Universe when we are working with intentions. The adventure is in staying awake and alert to be observant about where we are in expectation. When we are in expectation we are out of creation. We are expecting something to happen outside of ourselves instead of creating it.

The point of creation is unlimited and always ever giving. So, the importance of staying awake and aware of all we are creating is imperative as we are consciously opening up to wider pathways of overflowing happiness and joy. To create our lives in a manner that honors us, and that honors the world, happens when we are living in divine alignment with the Universe.

We have the ability to create joy, create happiness, create abundance and so much more. Spirit only wants for us to live in the overflow, for us to create with ease and joy. Let us embrace the tool of intention and get about doing just that.

Let me be clear here about the two different kinds of expectations. Expectations that are natural enhance our lives. Years ago, when I first began my intentional spiritual journey, a very dear friend of mine gave me a book as a goodbye present. I was moving out of the area to pursue my dream of acting. She placed a large bill in a wonderful book, and the stickers that held the bill in place read, "Expect the Best." Now, these little reminders gave me hope on my journey, they fueled me with anticipation of all the good that would be taking place on my adventure.

For years I left that bill in there, just so I could be reminded of the all-knowing power of Spirit and the many ways it supports me so generously. Those stickers reminded me to expect the best for my journey, and I did just that. As I did expect all good, that is what my experience was. Now if I had expected that I would get a job in 30 days and be a big star within a year, that could have led to disappointment. Do you see where I am headed? Instead, my intention was to create endless opportunities for success in work and be available for all that the Universe led me to do. In this way, I was open to the good of the Universe, not just what my limited mind saw as all good. No expectation here. This was intentional living.

So, the expectations I am referring to that lead to disappointment are the ones that are dependent on someone outside of us doing something we believe they should do for us, or a circumstance being just a certain way that WE want it.

When we look out into our world and have an expectation of how it should be (catch those two words, *how* and *should*!), then we are often in unconscious expectation. Hence, the importance of setting intentions to keep us out of dependent expectations. This detail is important for creating a life of intentional living. We must stay conscious and co-create so that we release the pattern of dependent expectation.

Expectation kills creativity, destroys connection and inhibits divine activity from coming through in a free-flowing manner. Hidden expectations exist everywhere and we often don't even know they exist. They are the little things that creep up in our consciousness when we allow it to go on autopilot. See if any of these ring a bell for you:

You experience upset if someone does not return your text or call fast enough.

When you receive a response you don't like, it angers you.

You will only have a good day if there's no traffic.

If your mate should compliment you, all would be well.

If anything MUST occur in the outside world to bring you happiness, then there lies an expectation. We cannot control when anyone is going to respond to us, be kind to us, tell us we look nice, thank us for our work—we cannot control any of these things. So, if we base our happiness on them, we are open to disappointment. The good news is we have the power to wake up, see it, change it and aim for living a life of intention, which releases all expectation.

You are now going to see how the power of your vision, language and intent can support you to stay connected to the Universal power of creation.

There is a way out, and the key to the kingdom is in your hand. The key to releasing expectation is living a life of bold intention.

⌇ REMEMBER ⌇

Take a breath, set your intention to release past expectations and choose to live a life of freedom!

CHAPTER 4

The Three Power Pillars

THERE IS A FLAWLESS RECIPE for creating intentions that bring forth powerful manifestations. When trying out a new recipe, for instance, it's necessary to have the right ingredients. Likewise, when you travel to a new place, you need your map or GPS. The same preparation goes into creating powerful intentions. The way in which you create your intentions is in direct proportion to how you manifest them. Think of it like this: the Universe can more easily support you when your intentions are clear and focused on what you wish to call forth. The clearer we are, the more accurately the GPS of Spirit can deliver what we are intending!

CLARITY IS POWER!

Clarity creates action, and when we create intentions with clarity, we infuse them with the power to unfold with momentum. There is a direct connection between clear intention and powerful manifestation. Most people miss this detail in building an intentional life. Let us not forget that there is great power in our words, as our words are energy in motion. So the importance of putting thought into the words we use in creating intentions cannot be spoken of too lightly. We have the ability to choose our words wisely, yet often we don't. We frequently say things without really thinking about what we are stating. (This is especially true when it comes to our inner chatter. We will deal with that in chapter 7.)

When we begin to realize the power of language, we can set the intention to stay alert to what words we are choosing to use when we speak! *Choice* is the key word here! We all have the power of choice, even when we pretend we don't. It is in our power to choose our direction so that our destination is determined with accuracy. It is in our choice of words and the energy behind those words, that allows the Universe to assist us to bring forth what we desire.

In keeping our language on track by writing powerful intentions, it is vitally important to activate the three pillars of creating clear intentions. This step is KEY! If you follow this recipe you will most definitely create intentions that are on track for full manifestation. These three pillars are the foundation of clear intention setting and will be your step-by-step guide in writing powerful statements of intent that will alter your reality. They are simple yet precise and potent. Activate and infuse your words with them and nothing will stop the Universe from responding to you in unlimited ways.

THE THREE POWER PILLARS OF INTENTIONS:

1. They must always be in the present moment

2. They must be positive

3. They must be based on spiritual qualities

We have to be clear when writing our intentions. Our ability to manifest our desires depends on it. I believe you will find these three pillars to be very helpful in guiding you. Follow this formula and you are bound for success! Your words will align with the vibration of creation and your fulfilled intentions will unfold before you.

1. THEY MUST ALWAYS BE IN THE PRESENT MOMENT

First and foremost, when we write intentions, they are always to be stated in the present moment. Our power to create comes to us in the present moment. We cannot go back and create in yesterday's moments, or tomorrow's moments. We cannot take a breath from yesterday or try to breathe for tomorrow. It is only at this moment that we can take a breath. The power resides in this moment alone! We can create at this moment and that is where our power lies. The power of choice, the power to create, the power to set our intentions, *all* are in the present moment. I cannot state this enough: be present to the present moment as you embark on living a life of intention. As you begin to write your intentions daily, a simple way to see if you are on track is to see if your language is in the present tense. So, here are some examples:

My intention is to begin my diet tomorrow.

My intention is to start eating healthier soon.

Versus:

My intention is to love my body in all the choices I make today.

My intention is to begin again, this day, this moment, to honor my body temple and take in foods that support excellent health.

Do you see the difference? The first two set you up for putting off the action, or momentum. The Universe will agree with you and keep your intention at bay and tomorrow will never come. Your focus will always be on tomorrow, not in the present. By staying in the present moment, and stating your intention in the NOW, you are immediately propelling the energetic field of creation into action. It is responding to you and your words. Activate your words with the present tense when writing and stating your intentions. Remember, clarity is power and the power is in the present moment!

2. THEY MUST BE POSITIVE

One day a client walked into my office so excited to tell me he had set his intention that day and he was feeling he had the swing of this intention setting! I was thrilled and asked him to share it with me. He then proceeded to say this:

"Here we go, you are going to love it! My intention is to NOT SMOKE!"

Now, first and foremost, I was thrilled he was beginning his journey by activating the most powerful tool to stay conscious in creating his life. So, first I acknowledged him for being present in his life by writing his intention for the day. I then asked a very important question. I asked if he was open for input on his intention. He laughed and said boldly, "Yes Kim, that is why I come to see you, I want your input!" I then reviewed with him the Three Pillars we had discussed before and asked if he felt he was in alignment with them in creating his intention. Quickly he realized that although his intention was aiming for what he wanted, it had a negative smack in the middle of it, and it also was stating what he DID NOT want! So, here is the thing: the Universe is listening to our words, and our intentions, and only wants to assist us to fulfill them. Although this man's intentions were clear that he did not want to smoke, the word *smoke* in itself was not needed in the intention. He was stating what he *did not want*, and the power resides in stating what we do want! So, in revising his intention I asked him if this would work: "My intention is to make choices that honor my body!"

With pure joy on his face, his YES was bold and clear. He got it. The power of the words may seem small in this example, yet they are so very potent and important in creating the results we want. It is of utmost importance to state what we desire, not what we are not wanting to create. It is also vitally important to utilize positive language and keep words like NOT out of our intentions!

Language has power, so let's be clear about using it in a powerful way. If you want positive results in your life, you must use language that carries that same positive vibration. Call forth what you wish for, and release what you do not wish to experience. Keep words such as NOT, DON'T, HATE and CAN'T out of your intentions. There are many other words to choose from, so get creative and let those guide you. Choose words that empower, uplift and are in the positive vibration, and you will receive back more positive energy. Keep your words positive. The power resides in your choice!

3. THEY MUST BE BASED ON POSITIVE QUALITIES

Often when I begin to teach this pillar a lot of people ask, "Just what does it mean to create intentions based on positive qualities?" In answering this question I invite you to think of it this way: You are aiming for the qualities you wish to experience more than the outcome you are naming. This does not mean we do not wish to experience divine outcomes, because we do. It means that if we are looking for an exact outcome or a certain result, then we may be limiting our intention. (Remember Chapter 3, Intention Vs. Expectation.) Our focus is on cultivating the qualities for the outcome to unfold naturally and in divine order. When we do that, the outcome follows exactly in divine order and usually in a more expansive way than we ever knew!

Let me give you an example. If you have to have a difficult conversation with someone you care about and you feel a lot of fear about having it, then you may find yourself unknowingly aiming for the other person to "be" a certain way. The way you want them to be. But you cannot control that, and you are setting yourself up for expectation again. In this certain situation, I would ask you what qualities you want to experience in the conversation. Maybe you would want to connect, to feel kindness and love and strength to speak openly. Then we would write an intention like this:

> My intention is to connect with my loved one as I lovingly stand in strength and open the door to deep levels of conversation and resolution.

Do you see how the qualities are what are leading the intention? The Universe can respond to this! We are still calling for a resolution, but we are open regarding how to get there! This is where the qualities of the intention are more meaningful to us than a prescribed outcome. We can always BE the qualities we wish to experience. As we own these and state them in our intentions, we are staying out of expectation and also allowing the Universe to assist in how it all unfolds. The blessing is that the Universe always brings us so much more than we ever knew. When we are basing our intentions on what we want to experience instead of just one result, then the Universe can have its way to deliver a bigger result than you ever knew possible!

This pillar takes practice and patience. Keep working with your intentions and remember to ask yourself what you want to feel, and then listen for the answer. You may have initially thought you wanted something from someone, but when you ask this question, you may find that you want to feel love, or connection or understanding. These are qualities you can activate in your intention work to create the flow and direction of what you wish to experience. These are qualities we can BE, and then we allow the outcomes to unfold without us directing. The *how* is up to the Universe, to the spiritual wisdom that guides us. It knows the how better than we do.

RELEASE THE HOW AND STAY IN THE NOW

The *how* is not our job. Letting go of the *how* is sometimes the most challenging aspect for individuals who utilize intentions, yet it is an absolute necessity. I often invite my clients to simply leave *how* out and surrender to the now. Remember, the power is in the present moment, and the *how* is up to the Universe. We only block ourselves when we go straight for needing to know *how* we are going to create something. In this practice, it is imperative to remember that when we aim to know *how* to do anything, we are considering only what we know we can do, or what we have seen someone else do. The Universe knows so much more! Knowing *how* to do something gives us a sense of control and safety, but it does not leave room for us to receive more than we knew possible.

When activating intentions, consider that the *how* will

be shown to you instead of you already knowing it. Be willing to think of it as an act of surrender. Surrendering to a power that has no limits whatsoever, and can miraculously deliver to you all that you are calling forth. There is safety and strength in knowing that this power wants only good for you and will respond to your willing and open heart. Your job is to release the *how* to stay in the now — and trust. You will be guided, you will be shown the path, and as you hold your clear intentions, you will be given the *how* at the perfect moment. Enjoy the journey!

ᴄᴏ **REMEMBER** ᴄᴏ

Take a deep breath and know that your practice and intention will give you the wisdom to follow through and give birth to what your heart has always known.

CHAPTER 5

The Pearls of the Journey

WE ALL HAVE A JOURNEY that is our own. Our journey is unique to ourselves, and individual to ourselves, and will most definitely look very different than anyone else's journey. Every single magnificent individual on the planet has their own personal adventure that is theirs to embark upon. And yes, that means YOU!

Our lives are a divine expression of our own path of unfoldment. Our journeys may look different in form and structure, yet there are universal qualities that are being birthed within each of us that determine the life path we are on. Notice that I said, "qualities" that are being birthed. Our life gives us unlimited opportunities to grow and expand, and when we are aware that to grow we must change, then the quality of our lives changes. Our intention in being spiritually awake and activating the fullest potential for our lives is to be conscious of our journey and to truly amplify the pearls that have come from it.

As I work with individuals who are waking up to the journey, when they can observe the path with a gentle heart of compassion, then they have an opportunity to evolve to a higher level of healing. Gentleness is the key to massive growth and expansion. As one practices releasing judgment they can then begin to describe themselves not by the story of their lives, but instead by who they had to become to move through that unique path. In other words, when this occurs, we open the door to the willingness to begin to cultivate the *pearls of the journey.*

We each have pearls that we have cultivated upon our path. Those pearls are the things, the qualities that had to be refined, practiced, honored and expanded in order for us to grow. We may have had enormous hardships to move through, and when we begin to be more interested in what had to be cultivated within us to move through those challenges, we then begin to find the pearls. In other words, when we become more interested in the pearls than staying stuck in the story, then we are on our growing edge and are ready to be more committed to who we have become!

Think of it like this: a pearl has to be rubbed with sand and go through a cleansing process to become the beautiful gem that we appreciate and love. While in the oyster shell, it is the irritation of sand that causes the agitation that creates the beauty of the pearl. It is the same for the pearls of our soul. Sometimes it is the agitation, the challenges, the difficult hardships that create an opening for us to embody qualities that have been dormant for too long. They exist within us but may need to be cultivated and amplified for us to move through certain tough times. To move through life challenges, we must grow. To grow, we become willing (hopefully, otherwise we go screaming and kicking!) to learn who we must become to move through the obstacles before us. This is where our own inner pearls become refined! Not easy, sometimes painful, but a necessary part of our growth and evolution!

Yesterday I was clever, so I wanted
to change the world. Today I am wise,
so I am changing myself.

Rumi

MY GROWING EDGE

A few years ago, I had a growth spurt that required massive strength and created a profound expansion in my life. I probably could not see it from that standpoint at the time I was in the thick of it, but looking back I am quite aware that I was being catapulted into expanding to the next level of the evolution of my soul. This catapulting action was at times extremely painful, at moments seemingly horrific, and completely impossible. Yet, it was clear that I was being called to grow, to expand and to evolve. I had to, actually. I CHOSE to activate every single spiritual practice I had in my toolbox to make it through to the other side.

The journey required me to live everything I knew, everything I believed in and everything I had ever learned. It was not comfortable, it was quite painful, and there were rivers of tears flowing while my pearls were being cultivated. Yet it was a necessary path that I had to take for my life to change. I will explore this more deeply in Chapter 6.

In this time of expansion, my spiritual teacher Michael Bernard Beckwith walked with me and lifted me when I would fall. He and my spiritual practitioner Kathleen McNamara would pick me up, help me dust myself off and then remind me of who I am. I remember so very clearly that Rev. Michael would look deep into my soul and ask, "What is your growing edge here, Kimberly? What must you grow into for you to get to the other side of this challenge?" He gently reminded me over and over again that the Universe was calling for me to grow.

An expansion of my soul was taking place in the midst of the challenge before me, and I was experiencing enormous growing pains. It was my job to remember that the Universe was backing me up, and it was necessary for me to be willing. I had to be willing to grow through the pain, and that is exactly what I chose, to grow in the midst of the darkness to get to the other side.

This term, "my growing edge," has served me for years, as even now I am always asking myself the same question that Rev. Michael asked me then. Since the Universe never stops, and the evolution of our souls does not stop urging us forward, you can see where this growing edge inquiry is so important! To evolve, we must stay curious about what growth spurts are necessary for us to expand. This expansion is needed for the continuing evolution of our soul. It has also served me quite well with my clients, as I ask them the same question. Sometimes they don't like it, yet it is a necessary one to ask.

"What is your growing edge?"

I am beyond clear that this question is imperative to ask. I know that the quality of our questions determines the quality of our lives, and it becomes necessary to ask often, "What is my growing edge?" This allows us to be propelled into discovering the gift within the challenge. Here is the kicker: what we are to become is the pearl of wisdom that must be birthed through us due to this challenge or circumstance! The pearl is the gift, and it can only come through YOU. It is your growing edge, but you must be willing to birth it.

The pearl is the gift and it must be birthed through you!

Our growing edge is that place where Spirit is stretching us. It is the quality, or qualities, that MUST be birthed, must be activated more fully to move through whatever challenge is before us. To be stretched is not such a bad thing. Stretching is good, just often uncomfortable. If we are willing to stay awake and conscious as we evolve, we will see where there is always an opportunity for growth in the midst of any challenge, any place that looks like a setback. I believe what comes to us as a setback is another moment for us to "sit back" and review, recalibrate and renew our choices and patterns. There is room to feel the sadness, the hurt or whatever else comes up on the journey, but we must allow it to come through us, and we do not need to stay in it forever. It comes up to be healed, to be loved, to be understood. Our intention is to understand, to grow and to know more fully who we are.

When we become more interested in who we are in our growing edge, then we see the certain qualities that had to be cultivated in order to grow through the challenge. I invite my clients to become more interested in "who" they became than the description of the story they have been living. Our intention must be to find the qualities of who we became, more than being interested in staying stuck in the pain of the story.

WHERE HAVE YOU GROWN?

Some people may grow in strength, in persistence, in faith or in endless other areas, but there is always a quality that had to be cultivated in order to make it through the challenge. I am interested in that. You must be interested in that. Every one of us has an opportunity to be on our growing edge, on that edge of transformation. We have the opportunity to be on our razor's edge with every encounter that we move through. When we can observe the path we have been upon with a gentle compassion, then we have the opportunity to look at who we had to become to move through that journey. We can choose to expand through the difficulties by cultivating the qualities that birth powerful pearls that change our lives forever. Consider this:

What qualities were necessary to embody before you were able to move through the challenging experiences?

_____

_____

_____

_____

_____

Be more interested in the qualities of who you became, than in staying stuck in your story!

When we are ready to let go and grow, then we no longer define ourselves by the story. This is the blessing that is absolutely beyond measure! Right there, that is the blessing that is masterful. When we are more interested in the pearls of who we became, we then begin to release the victim mentality, the story of, "Well, this happened to me, that is why I am like this," which is all just justification. We must become more interested in what was necessary for us to grow. Your narrative may then sound like this: "I grew in patience, I grew in strength, I grew this muscle of unstoppable faith during that hardship, and that muscle now prepares me for the next adventure in my life." Letting go of the story does not mean we do not honor our participation in it. Instead, our let-go is the freedom to not be bound by it! We are more than our story!

This is when the story loses its power. When the story loses its power, we then stand strong with the ability to move forward in a profoundly expansive way. We honor the pearls of wisdom that we gained and we amplify our evolution to the next level of what we came here to be. I want to be more interested in that than being stuck in the descriptive of the story of how I got here. The story just becomes the details. It may be fun to tell the story, but it is just a story! Those are the details of the journey; they do NOT determine what will occur now, unless you let them. We always have a choice of what we DO. Even if the choice is hard, it is what we apply when the obstacles get bigger than we ever thought they would that matters. That is when our spiritual muscle gets activated. When we look back at those moments, then we can see where we took the opportunity to choose to evolve to the next level of our brilliance!!!! A powerful place to be indeed!

I invite you to ask yourself on a regular basis, "What gift within me is seeking to emerge in this situation?" "What is my growing edge here?" Place your attention on the emerging gift rather than the challenge at hand, and you will witness how the weight of the challenge begins to dissolve.

Let us choose now to be much more interested in cultivating the pearls of wisdom than being stuck in anything of the past that no longer serves us.

You can honor your journey, honor the steps that got you here and bless the expansion even if it was uncomfortable. Bless it and move onward. That is your charge!

⌒ REMEMBER ⌒

Take a deep breath, release your story
and reclaim your life.

CHAPTER 6

Cracking the Shell, My Journey

IT IS IMPORTANT to share my own journey so you may understand more fully how to apply this practice. The important point I would like to express here is that it is only my intention to share my story for the purpose of teaching. In no way am I a victim to the story. I have grown past that (thank goodness) and can share the journey and consider all the cultivated pearls that were birthed in me during that time. In addition to revealing the pearls that were discovered, I wish to share with you the important practices that I lived, that I embodied, for these practices allowed my pearls to be birthed!

MY JOURNEY

There was a period in my life, a specific five-year time span, that had more challenges in it than I would have thought possible. I am highly aware that this five-year stretch of my life created a safe haven for me to grow exponentially. Not just grow, but truly grow in a way that I never thought possible. I had to expand beyond my present view or knowledge of myself. I did not think it was conceivable before this time began that I could ever grow in the manner I did. I did not know I had it in me.

Fifteen years into my marriage it became very clear to me that the partnership was causing enormous harm to my children and to me. It took years to come to a clear understanding of what had to be done, and in those years, I never stopped trying everything I could to heal through the harm. Through much prayer and the practice of every tool that I had, it became clear that it was necessary for the marriage to be dissolved. When I say that I practiced every tool that I had and that I teach, it is not an understatement. These tools saved my life. They were my life, my very existence.

It all began as a time of deep prayer and bold intention to receive clarity. I was seeking guidance to know what steps to take with the challenges that were before me. For years my marriage was not healthy, harm was being done and no matter which way I applied patience, acceptance, and deeper levels of communication, it didn't shift the intense anger and upset my husband was expressing. I prayed and prayed and set intentions for divine clarity, and then more intentions for strength to implement the clarity when it came through. I chose to grow in willingness to listen so expansively that I did not react from my place of hurt, but from a place of truly listening for the highest good to be revealed. I was consciously choosing to stay in my practice and lovingly respond even when it was harder than anything I had ever been through. I was determined to hear the sweet whisperings of Spirit's guidance that was much more profound than any human condition. With every prayer, I released reactionary patterns that I had utilized prior to that time, and set my intentions to stand in calm response to the situation at hand.

So, after years of practice, intending to find the highest choice for all concerned in my family, it became very clear that the marriage was to end. Once that was decided, the intensified five-year span of hurricane-size challenges ensued. I thought it had been hard prior to that moment, but the storm broke with new intensity.

During that five-year time, more things occurred than any book could hold. (I did not want to write *Gone with the Wind*!) But, the most important insight I caught was that it was imperative for me to survive and thrive, so I had to grow. Not just a little growth spurt; an evolutionary jump was necessary. I had to be willing to live on my growing edge, and amplify all the tools in my toolbox.

Faith was my guiding light and powerful intention. I chose to have faith in the unseen because if I tried to figure out the *how* I was going to move through the challenges before me, I never would have been able to catch even a glimpse of what was in store. It was clear that I needed more than the knowledge I had accumulated to get through what was before me. I had to expand and trust Spirit more than ever before. I had to be willing to stretch, to lean into spiritual wisdom and live in unstoppable faith, listening until I caught instruction for what step to take next. I chose to listen for inner guidance with each step and move through situations that seemed unbearable.

> *The obstacle in the path becomes the path.*
>
> Ryan Holiday

When my 20-year marriage ended I was totally blindsided by my husband's animosity. Overnight, I was a single mom with absolutely no support. I found myself pulling finances out of thin air and meeting my children's needs while standing firm as rage and hatred were thrown at me. I had to figure out how to put food on the table, and tend to children needing medical attention and emotional support. It was not a smooth transition but I had to hold myself together so my children had a place to lean into and feel some safety in the middle of the storm. In the midst of it all, I was falling apart inside. I was so very scared. I was terrified, but I kept moving forward.

Through the fear, I kept staying in intention, committed to being present and conscious, and moving onward. I took A LOT of deep breaths! I remembered Rev. Michael saying, "If the fear will not subside, just pick it up and take it with you. Just keep staying in faith and moving forward."

My intention is to stand in unstoppable faith
as I face all that comes before me.

Life changed overnight. I suddenly was thrown into handling the house mortgage completely on my own. At that point in my career, my private practice was fewer hours a week than even part-time; I had maybe six or seven ongoing clients. It appeared that I did not have a strong enough financial base at that moment to afford a mortgage, medical needs for my two kids and a family of dogs and horses to boot! My income did not even cover one of those things at that time. Believe me when I say I was praying with every breath!

The financial burdens were massive and growing, and my income did not match the needs. There were many days I had no idea where I would get $20 to buy some milk, eggs and bread for my children or food for the animals, but I kept my intention and kept praying. Tears were falling, but I kept my practice and aimed forward, committed to finding solutions where there seemed to be none.

Somehow we made it through the winter holidays even though finances were slim. My parents and friends were my support system. They brought food, picked up my kids from school if I was working and always reminded me I would get through this. Friends came over just to help me hang curtains on the windows and carry in a garden table for us to have a place to have dinner.

Then the first of the year came and I thought it would be a new beginning. I was committed to growing my business to create more financial security and to finding solutions for my children's needs. I felt like January would bring new possibilities. Yet, the following five weeks of that new year brought only bigger challenges and opportunities to practice what I knew. I will review the first five weeks of the year with you, and it will give you an idea of what the entire five-year time span was like.

It was the first weekend of January, my son Lucas's birthday. He was headed out to his first motocross competition and I was to meet him there. He and his friend had gone a day early to practice and learn the track. My excitement to be able to do this with my son for his birthday was overwhelming. It had been a tough few months and this would bring him so much joy. I was only five minutes down the road on Pacific Coast Highway when the phone rang and his friend told me there had been an accident and that Lucas was in an ambulance on the way to the hospital. I hung up the phone, wiped the tears from my face and began sending him prayers. Prayers for his healing and wholeness, while surrounding his body temple with light and blessing the doctors and the staff of the hospital. I then set my intention to arrive safely and quickly, even though I had no idea where I was headed. All the while, I sent my son love and strength.

A few hours later, I walked into the ER and found him lying there looking defeated. His hurt and sadness were palpable. The doctors said he was lucky that he only had a mild concussion and needed to rest for a couple of weeks. Answered prayer for sure! Back home we went, broken motorcycle and healing son, all prayers and intentions fulfilled!

The next weekend came and the kids were not back from school yet when I returned home from my meetings. I decided to walk down to the barn to check on the horses. Dusty and Rascal had been with us for years and were part of the family. Dusty was my daughter's paint mare and Rascal was my big gelding. As I walked toward the barn I saw Rascal but no Dusty, which was odd.

Two steps into the center aisle of the barn I looked to my right and found her. She was upside down, lodged between a pipe corral fence and a retaining wall. The space was maybe only two and a half feet in width from the pipes to the rock wall. Her legs were in the air, her head was turned to the side stuck under the last pipe. It was a terrifying sight and fear screamed through my body as I ran to her. She was in shock and clearly could not move. I had no idea how long she had been there. I had last seen her when I fed her breakfast and she was fine, but that was hours before. I had no idea how she could have gotten out of her stall and fallen upside down in this very small area. It all seemed so impossible, but the how was not my concern at that point; the priority was to get her out. Or could I?

There seemed to be no way she could survive; there was no seemingly way to get her dislodged. But those thoughts were not an option for me at that moment. My teaching and practice took me to what I knew how to do best. I immediately went to her face, rubbed her and told her to hold on. I promised we would get her out and I was going to get help. I prayed with her, a fast and laser-focused prayer before I ran to the house to grab the phone.

My first call was to my dear friend Joanie, who lived around the corner and was a horsewoman. She said she was on her way and I then called 911, as I needed the fire department and I needed them fast! I was calling and running back to the barn to be at Dusty's side. I wiped her face and kept talking to her and begging her to hold on. I was not giving up on her.

Within moments I looked up and my friend Joanie was walking slowly toward us, but I noticed she seemed hesitant and was not removing her sunglasses. She later told me she made a choice to not remove her glasses, as she did not want me to see her eyes filled with tears as she did not believe this could end well. I immediately grabbed Joanie's hands and I began praying so loudly the entire block could have heard. I did not care. I was sobbing but my words were clear: I was calling for a miracle and that somehow, some way, this little horse would be lifted out of this predicament and we would be guided on how to help her best. At the last word, "AMEN," I looked at my friend and said, "Let's get to work!"

In the moments that followed, I am clear we were guided as to what to do. Divine guidance was operating through both of us.

We created a handoff situation where I would gently and carefully reach down between Dusty's four legs and slowly remove the large stones that had fallen upon her belly and then hand them to Joanie. My head was only inches away from her powerful hoofs. I then began to remove the stones that were holding up the retaining wall, trying to get to dirt, and create more space for her. Soon there was enough room for her to wiggle her head out from under the pipe, and the stones near her shoulder area were almost removed to expose the dirt.

When she began to feel this wee bit of spaciousness, she did not hesitate to try to move. I panicked a bit as I thought it was too soon and she was going to hurt herself more. But she was determined and somehow had a burst of strength. I was screaming, "No Dusty, wait girl," but she ignored my pleas and did something I will never forget. Neither will my friend Joanie. This feisty little girl wanted to live, thank God!

We watched her contort her body in a way that was shocking. It seems that by us removing the stones near her shoulders she was given more space to twist her upper body to the side and plant her two front hoofs into the dirt wall. This momentum then allowed her to use those hoofs to push her a bit up toward the opening and feel some freedom. Then she twisted her front half in such a manner that I thought she was going to break a leg. Clearly, she knew best! She kept at it and the next thing we knew she twisted her back half to try to catch up with her upper body and get free of the space she was stuck in. As I was crying and holding onto my dear friend, this little miracle horse used every muscle she had to physically do the impossible . . . and she stumbled to her feet! She was standing, quite wobbly, but she was standing!

I wrapped my arms around her neck and kept saying, "Thank you, thank you, thank you!" This was divine action manifested and I knew it. The impossible had occurred before our eyes and I was in shock and overwhelming gratitude at the same time. She kept standing, shaky, her body beaten up and bloody, but she was standing!

I looked up, and at that moment the fire department was walking through the yard! It was hard to describe what we had just witnessed, but they were catching pieces of it and taking in our expansive joy at that moment. It ended well and our tears were for gratitude! Answered prayer at its best!

That was weekend number two of that year and we were headed into weekend number three.

The third weekend of January my 13-year-old daughter, Lila, was in the midst of preparing for a school play performance that was a week away. I went to pick her up from dress rehearsal on a Saturday afternoon and when I got there she ran out and asked if she could please spend the night at a friend's house. I hesitated as I didn't know this family very well so I wasn't sure about the details. The mother met me and assured me that the girls would get lots of rest because they had another full-dress rehearsal the next day. She reassured me that she would bring them back to the school in the morning. So, I went home to rest as it was my first evening alone in weeks. The house was quiet and I was taking it in.

Then, close to 10:00 p.m., the phone rang. I picked it up and I could hear screams at the other end. Then I heard the voice of the mother I had met only hours earlier. She was panicked and saying Lila had been hurt badly, that somehow, she fell through a window. (What I didn't know was that it was a plateglass window on the third floor of their apartment, and somehow she stopped her fall and they had to pull her back in.) Then, what you always hope doesn't happen: the phone went dead! Lost reception and all I had were those few sentences and I knew it wasn't good.

For a very brief moment in time, I stood in my living room and took a massive deep breath and as the tears fell I began the first words of prayer and simultaneously went into motion. I began grabbing clothes and throwing them into a bag. Not sure where I might be for the night or what Lila would need. I was just grabbing things and praying out loud, all the while pushing the code to call back the number that had just called me.

Suddenly a male voice answered and asked, "Are you the mother of this young girl?" I answered yes and above the screams I could hear him introduce himself as the fire captain. He told me that she was cut up pretty badly and I better get to the hospital as soon as possible. The last thing he said to me was, "Ma'am, you might need to call the plastic surgeon, she is cut up bad." Again, I jumped into the car and began racing in the night to an unfamiliar hospital.

As I drove alone through the darkness, I kept breathing and praying, setting my intentions, just as I had with Lucas. I was sending my precious daughter strength and love, and blessing the doctors, the ambulance, the nursing staff and blessing her beautiful body temple. I just kept practicing, and driving quickly through the night. Thank goodness Siri got me there. I jerked the car into a spot and ran into the emergency room. I was greeted by a nice receptionist who asked me to take a seat, but all I remember is the firmness in my voice when I said, "There's no way in hell

I'm sitting down, please show me where my daughter is!" As if by magic, a nearby door opened and a big powerful male nurse popped his head out and motioned me toward him. I saw my daughter through the door and all I could see was her face stained with tears and her arms in the air with bandages drenched in blood. I ran in and held her while we both wept.

The nurse told me they had changed the bandages in the ambulance and again at the hospital because the blood was coming so fast. They soon got her a room, began to clean her up and give her some pain medicine so she could rest.

By 2:30 in the morning the doctor began to numb her arms so he could start stitching. She had over 40 stitches, mostly in her arms with a few on the back of her legs. Seems Lila had stopped her fall when she had been pushed backward into the glass that night. A game of wrestling on a bed had turned dangerous!

I am forever grateful that somehow she had stopped her fall with her fingers wrapped around the window and half her body out of it before she was pulled back in. A miracle indeed, and she knew it. She kept telling me that something was holding her and keeping her from falling from that third-floor window onto the concrete below. She knew she was being held!

The drive home at 4:30 in the morning and putting her to bed as the sun came up was indescribable. As she got into bed, she muttered some words of love and appreciation as she fell into an exhausted sleep. I just stood there, a bit numb, yet again, aware of this overwhelming gratitude that we were on this side of it and her body would heal. My daughter was home, and tears of gratitude fell down my cheeks and to the floor. We slept for a few hours before those darn bandages needed changing again.

I'm proud to say that that courageous daughter of mine still performed the following weekend! They had to make a slight costume adjustment to cover the bandages on her arms, but that beautiful soul set her intention to be on the stage and perform, and she did just that! After the show on that fourth weekend of January, we all took a deep breath.

Then the first weekend of February came, and Lucas had been released by the doctor to ride again. He promised to be safe as he was out the door on a little dirt bike adventure with a friend. I was home alone and in the barn putting medicine on Dusty's wounds. She was still healing from all the road rash she took that day when she was caught in that tight spot, but she was healing and we were so very grateful. My mind was wandering when suddenly I heard Lucas's voice in my head say, "Mom, you're not to believe this, I just got in another motorcycle accident." I dismissed the mind chatter, finished with Dusty and walked to the house.

Moments later the phone rang, and it was Lucas. Whether it was a premonition or a foreshadowing of what was to be, I do not know, but the conversation I had in my head moments before came to life now on the phone with him. He let me know he was not hurt bad but had had a fall and there was quite a bump on his shoulder. He was headed to urgent care.

Now inside my head, I kept hearing, "Are you kidding me? Did this seriously just happen? What is going on?" By this time I was a pro at knowing what was next. Say a prayer, set my intention, grab my purse, jump in the car. Within 20 minutes I was there with him and was just grateful it wasn't too bad. His body would heal; it was his heart I was concerned about.

In the midst of divorce, this was Lucas's outlet, his place to go forget it all. He was a brilliant rider and these accidents were not in alignment with his ability. I reminded him that is why they are called "accidents" and that maybe it was time for him to take a break for a while until things were a little smoother. He agreed, and so did his body.

The following weekends over the next few months, I told my children they would be wrapped in bubble wrap if they attempted to leave the house. Seriously! We had experienced enough 9-1-1 calls for a lifetime!

AFTER THE STORM

There would be more challenges coming my way, but I was committed to standing in faith, living my practice and not succumbing to fear. I knew that even though I felt so alone and scared at times, there was a presence in me that was bigger than any challenge before me. I had direct access to the wisdom of the Universe, I just had to continue to listen and surrender to the divine guidance I was being given. I was absolutely committed to living what I knew and practicing with every breath. I set intentions countless times a day. I did not walk into any situation without preparing myself and connecting to Spirit. My intentions gave me strength to carry on and they fueled the Universe with my desires so that I could co-create powerfully. I prayed, and I kept moving forward.

The year continued onward and a few more surprises rose up. In the following months, things occurred that gave me more opportunities to work my practices and stand in the intention of unstoppable faith. I set my intention to find solutions, swallowed my pride and, with the help of friends, I was able to save a home for us in the community where my kids had grown up.

In the following months and years, life only continued to keep unfolding in many ways that I never saw coming. But what I do know is this, the two things that saved my life were my commitment to my spiritual practice and my loving and compassionate support system that walked with me through the dark night of my soul. My practice and my support system, that is what kept me walking through the storm.

The brighter day did come, solutions came forth and countless moments of fulfilled intention continued to be revealed. My business kept growing, my children kept healing and more miracles than I could count appeared, always at the most divine moment.

During the crossroads of my life, two necessary ingredients were present, and I invite you to consider amplifying them when you are in the midst of challenges and transformation. It is imperative to stand in WILLINGNESS and TRUST if you wish the highest good to be revealed in your life. I had to be willing to trust even when I did not see any evidence of solutions in the circumstances before me. Yes, it may feel like you are walking a tightrope, but this is your growing edge! The tightrope is being held by the Universe, so keep walking!

You gain strength, courage and confidence by every experience in which you really stop to look fear in the face. You are able to say to yourself, "I lived through this horror. I can take the next thing that comes along."

Eleanor Roosevelt

You must be willing to embody your practice of intention even when it is hard — especially when it is hard! Your intention is the seed of the transformation that you desire to experience! And don't forget your toolbox for the journey.

TRUST, SET YOUR INTENTION AND LET GO!

I now can say with every cell in my body that I am grateful for that journey. From this standpoint, I am choosing to be grateful forevermore, as I continue to discover the pearls of that journey. The pearls were worth the pain. I can honestly say that. Don't know that I would have ordered it up, but on this side, I can truly say I am so grateful to be the woman I am today because of the pearls I cultivated upon a very difficult journey. No matter how much pain your journey caused, no matter how difficult it was to get through, choose to move forward with unstoppable faith.

∽ REMEMBER ∾

Take a deep breath and boldly embrace the wisdom of your journey with gratefulness and gratitude.

CHAPTER 7

Train of Transformation

GET ON BOARD, we are headed down the track of transformation. I must forewarn you, if you begin (which I know you will) to put these principles and tools into practice and to live a life of powerful intention, you have a 100% guarantee that your life will transform. The question is, are you ready for that? I ask if you are ready because transformation can sometimes be messy. Not always, but very often things tend to get shaken up before they are ready to transform into something greater.

> *A genuine intention to transform is an invitation for spiritual lightning to strike and reveal our self-sabotaging habits, pointing us in the direction of what must be released so that we may evolve into our next dimension of being!*
>
> Michael Bernard Beckwith

We must be willing to let go of the old patterns, old thought habits and old beliefs and allow the awakening of Truth to transform our lives. So, I ask again, are you ready for that? I can tell you from my personal experience that the ride is truly worth whatever shake-up might happen along the way. Living a life of pure intentional alertness, one that is truly open to receiving the highest good at all times, is a transformation that is worth saying yes to. The many unlimited blessings that will be showered upon you are mind-boggling and life-changing and worth the ride!

My intention is to be willing to release anything that no longer serves me so that I may surrender to the inner transformation of my soul and fully experience my highest good!

The basis of true transformation begins with a clear intention to let go. To transform, we must be willing to let go and expand beyond the present paradigm we find ourselves in. Transformation requires shifting out of limiting thinking to expansive knowing. It is necessary to be fully present and awake so we remain available to live what we know in the present moment. To make a bold shift, we must be conscious and open to shifting out of any past limited thinking. Our intention must be to stay in the present, trust the journey and be willing to consistently let go, as these are all vitally important keys on the pathway of profound transformation.

Transformation: A dramatic change
in form or appearance.

Oxford English Dictionary

We are on an ongoing and never-ending journey of outgrowing our structures and expanding the parameters of what we know. From the moment we were born and took our first breath, we have been growing and changing. As we are born into a body, and I am assuming you have been if you are reading this, then you know the body is constantly changing. In the midst of these changes, we are mostly unaware of all that our bodies are dealing with and are handling for us.

If we took the time to focus on and appreciate the detailed structure of functionality that our bodies perform with ease, as well as the ways in which our body naturally changes, we may see that it is necessary for us to allow the changes in our thinking to adjust with the same smoothness.

Our bodies serve us well. They are the precious and powerful instruments by which we have the human experience. We must be willing to let go of what we know to grow and experience more. It is always about experiencing more, not less. We grow to know life more fully, and a necessary element of consciously growing is consistently letting go. To grow, we must let go! They go hand in hand. Therefore, the importance of living a life of powerful intention is an imperative on the path of transformation. The key to accepting, embracing and moving through the challenges, the transformations in life, is to embody the practice of intention.

Our intentions guide us through our transformative process so we are able to not only survive, but also glide and grow through every change that comes before us!

With every breath, we can choose to let go of the familiar, the road we have already traveled, while knowing that the next step into the unknown is already paved for us. The Universe awaits our willingness to trust the unseen, to go deep in consciousness and allow our connection to lift us out of any appearance of muck that we have been stuck in. Know that when we courageously choose to let go and grow, we are inviting Spirit to guide us, to direct us to higher ground. It may feel scary, the terrain may feel rocky and dangerous, and it may appear that possibly remaining stuck would be less painful. A limiting thought is only a pattern of habit. Ultimately, staying stuck causes much more pain.

We always have power over our habitual thought patterns, which keep us small, and we must activate that power. It is a muscle that we can choose to cultivate, the muscle of deep trust and knowing that more is always coming, so the intention is to expand our container to hold more of life.

To do this, to create space for more good than we have ever imagined, our letting go of whatever does not serve us is imperative.

You just decide, once and for all, to take the journey by constantly letting go.

Michael A. Singer, *The Untethered Soul*

CHANGE REQUIRES SHIFTING

It takes courage and strength to shift out of limiting thinking into expansive knowing and growing. We are called to think big, to widen our horizons from what we have known up until this point and accept there is more to experience. There is more to know than we may be able to see from the present standpoint. In other words, our vision is limited by where we are standing at any given moment. To trust the process of transformation, we must be willing to allow the vision of Spirit to guide us when we cannot see past where we are. It requires us to be willing to be MORE than we presently know ourselves to be. This takes enormous courage!

There are many teachers of this philosophy, yet one in particular stands out above the rest. This teacher exemplifies great strength and mastery in the process of transformation. I am convinced that this specific teacher knows transformation better than any other being on the planet, and yet this masterful one typically grows no more than an inch in length and weighs less than half an ounce. This great sage offers us their life as the perfect example of what true intention to transform looks like. This wise master is the magnificent caterpillar.

Let's look at the journey of a caterpillar for a moment so that we may fully understand the willingness of these brilliant and tender beings. From the very scientific point of reference, when a caterpillar goes into its chrysalis state it is not such a pretty picture.

First, the caterpillar digests itself, releasing enzymes to dissolve all of its tissues. In this process, it literally digests itself internally and reduces itself to a gooey consistency, or the consistency of soup. During that time there are certain organized groups of cells known as imaginal discs that survive the digestive process. At that point, it grows a disc for each of the adult body parts it will need as a mature butterfly, discs for its eyes, wings, its legs and so on.

Once the caterpillar has disintegrated all of its tissues, except for the discs, those imaginal discs use the protein-rich soup all around them to fuel the rapid cell division required to form the wings, the antennae, legs, eyes, genitals and all the other features of an adult butterfly. A profound process, to say the least: nature at its best!

The lesson to remember is that just like the caterpillar,

everything is within you to assist you through your own transformational process.

It is important to note that getting a look at this metamorphosis is difficult, as disturbing a caterpillar inside its cocoon or chrysalis risks botching the transformation. The lesson is, we are not to disturb the process of letting go and birthing the next evolution of the sweet caterpillar. Again, let us reflect on this in our own lives. Our own inner transformation can be botched and blocked as well if we disturb the process midway through or decide it is too difficult and back out before we are completely through our unique growth expansion. Our willingness to let go is imperative if we are to allow our inner transformation to take place.

We must be fearless like the caterpillar and press on even when the growing pains are intense! On the other side of the growing edge of this precious being, wings to fly are being constructed and perfected! (Credit to *Scientific American*, writer Ferris Jbir, Aug. 10, 2012.)

As you can see, the caterpillar's transformation is not the beautiful fairytale version that many of us have been led to believe. But the important note to take from this lesson is that the caterpillar was willing to take the journey because it was worth it! To fly, to grow wings and have the freedom to soar was worth the full-on breakdown and rebuilding of its entire body structure. Do our own lives not deserve the same importance? Can we be as courageous and resilient as this small miracle is and let go of so much, only to be transformed into so much more? I invite you to take the risk and embody the wisdom of the caterpillar as you surrender to your own inner transformation.

TRANSFORMATIONAL WIGGLE

Years ago, I was speaking on stage about this beautiful caterpillar phenomenon and I began to make reference to the process, calling it the transformational wiggle. That is because what I did not mention above is there is a point when the caterpillar goes to break down his entire body structure into goo that he puts him/herself into a massive wiggle. This is necessary for the breakdown of the entire structure so that it can digest itself. So, imagine this masterful being putting itself into a massive shakedown, a wiggle of all wiggles, with the intention of demolishing its own structure to digest itself to grow wings to fly. Wow, is all I have to say. Talk about willingness and surrendering to a higher state of being! It is a beautiful thing to contemplate. So, back to that evening when I was speaking of this. I literally began to wiggle on stage and invited all those there to join me! I asked everyone to take on a new viewpoint of the seeming challenges in their lives. What would be possible if they connected the challenge with an opportunity for a "transformational wiggle"? The room got it and lightened up and agreed that from that point onward, all would be willing to dance and wiggle when challenges came before them. The "transformational wiggle" came to be!

To this day, I still receive posts and notes from clients sharing their time of intense challenges, and how they chose to take a stand for a big transformational wiggle. They now welcome their shakedown because they know that on the other side of it, they will be given wings to fly!

Transformation requires shifting out of limiting thinking to expansive knowing.

Where must we expand if we are choosing to embrace true transformation in our lives? What must we cultivate to be powerfully willing to change and grow? As the caterpillar teaches us, change is not always easy, yet with the proper tools, we may just wiggle our way right through it. To move through a transformation with more grace and less pain, it is necessary to intentionally cultivate these qualities:

Courage

Resiliency

Trust

Flexibility

Self-love

COURAGE

My intention is to courageously move forward in my life!

Courage is a choice! I love courageous people. I think courage is sexy and magnificent. Superheroes possess courage, and each and every one of us is a superhero in our own making. So, we each have courage built into our cells, illuminated in our bloodstream. Courage is something we must call forth and practice as often as possible. Even though it is built within us, right in our DNA, many of us hang out in the fear zone and keep our courage in lockdown. But it is there, awaiting the door to be opened so it can be set free!

Courage is something we activate in the face of fear. We begin by not avoiding fear, but consciously choosing to move through it. We may be standing in a fearful situation, yet we can choose to move through the fear, not be stopped by it. In all situations, we can take a breath, inhale courage, exhale fear and take the necessary step forward. We may be shaking in our boots, but so does the master teacher.

Let us wiggle our way through fear and embrace our courage with strength.

RESILIENCY

My intention is to be resilient and unshakable in my determination as I create my life on purpose!

Resiliency is being able to stand up after the journey has knocked you down, to stand up again and again and stay the course even when you may not see the finish line. Resilient people are unshaken by circumstance. They see the bumps in the road, the challenges ahead, and they choose to be unstoppable. Resilient individuals do not let fear stop them. They may pick the fear up and carry it with them if they have to, but they do not get stopped by the fear.

Resiliency has been defined as the ability to withstand or recover quickly from difficult conditions. Our ability to recover, to honor ourselves and heal our hurts, to stay alert to the path of self-love, allows us to build resiliency.

All of us have the ability to be resilient; we must choose to practice it.

TRUST

My intention is to surrender to deep trust, to know I am guided and supported with every breath I take.

To transform, the key element is trust! One must have unstoppable faith to be willing to transform when it is evident it may be difficult and even painful.

Trust is the very first tool we were blessed with when we came into this body temple. When we took our first breath, we unconsciously trusted it was safe to exhale as there was enough of what we needed to inhale and exhale. Our very first teaching of trust was our breath! It was in our birth instructions: just keep breathing! Inhale and exhale, there was always more to inhale as we let go of every exhale. WE TRUSTED and kept breathing without even thinking about it! This is profound evidence that trust is our first practice and we do it naturally. Yet, somewhere along the journey of life, we may have lost our natural ability to trust that all would work out for our highest good, always.

Today, may we contemplate back to our very first lesson in trust and begin again to breathe with a deep sense of trust that there is more than enough to inhale and exhale.

Let us consciously choose to build the muscle of trust that we were blessed with at birth.

FLEXIBILITY

My intention is to master flexibility and fluidity and move through life with grace and abundant joy!

Flexibility creates fluidity! Fluidity opens the door and allows the possibility to take up space. To move through all of life's joys and challenges, we must be flexible so as to not be taken down by circumstances. When we are rigid, we can stumble and crack and collapse in the midst of life experiences. Being stiff, confined, stuck in one viewpoint creates a lot of rigid patterns that limit our experience with the unlimited nature of the Universe! Yet the opposite of rigidity is flexibility.

Think of gymnasts. They have trained their bodies to be fluid, bendable and in motion as they exhibit the impossibility of what our bodies can do. When we choose to be flexible and fluid, we are choosing to surrender to something bigger than our own thinking, to have its way with us.

We may not be able to fully understand how all we desire will manifest through us, yet our intention to be flexible to life's changes, to embody spiritual wisdom, will give us the grace to move forward into the unseen.

Always remember: sometimes the unseen will reveal miracles to us at any moment!

SELF-LOVE

My intention is to make choices that honor who I am as I practice deep levels of self-love!

Self-love stands for soul serenity, and it is a most beautiful thing. Mastering self-love is an art, and it has nothing to do with puffing up the ego. Let me be clear: to love oneself is not an egoic sensation, but instead a revelation of a deep appreciation of our life as a spiritual being. Being grateful that we have this life, this body, to awaken and be of high service.

To be of the highest service to others, we must begin with self-love. Very often when we talk about love, we consider how we can be more loving to others. How we can speak more kindly, share our thoughts from the heart and search for ways to express kindness to those in our life that we love so very much. But rarely do we consider how we can be more loving to ourselves. Practicing being kinder to ourselves is not something we usually make a priority, yet it is imperative we start now. Amplifying self-love is a spiritual practice and the more loving we are to ourselves, the more loving we are to the world. To be a kind and loving individual, we must begin within our own soul with learning to embody expansive acts of self-love.

A bold intention to love oneself and honor oneself through all of life's journey is a glorious thing!

These are the qualities that prepare us to stay open and available to inner transformation. Cultivating them creates the space to allow the necessary shifts to occur with grace and strength. We are evolving beings, and change is a requirement of evolution. Transformations assist in the evolution of our souls. We must let go of whatever is keeping us in limitation. We cannot expect our outer situations to change while we remain the same inwardly. It is necessary to remember that transformation is an inward journey, one of self-discovery, self-acceptance and self-empowerment. We become more of who we truly are when we are willing to transform.

Let us live a life of passion, to fulfill our dreams and visions, by choosing to allow our inner transformations to propel us forward.

So, I ask you, what is your catalyst for transformation? Are you ready to courageously step out beyond your comfort zone, let go of what does not serve you and step onto the train of transformation? The fuel to lift your intentions is depending on your willingness to transform. The time is NOW!

I believe if you are here reading this, you are ready to transform. Waiting holds no value. If you truly know you have the tools, matched with the willingness and the guidance and support of the Universe, you are ready!

You came here to live full out, to fulfill your destiny, to live your highest expression and deliver your gifts with unbridled joy. We cannot stay in the past and live our passion because our growth is directed by our vision. Live your passion, and allow the transformational wiggle to begin!

Life is lived on the edge!
Will Smith

When we are willing to stand on the edge of our transformation, we are preparing to soar. We shall have the faith to know that as we dive deep into our transformational work, that Spirit will give us wings to fly! We will be given wings to fly or a bridge to walk upon, but we shall soar to new heights of expansion that will uplift our lives in miraculous ways!

My intention is to be willing to be transformed by this moment and surrender to the awakening of my soul.

Consider this beautiful and insightful expression from Marianne Williamson, on transformation:

It's when we face the darkness squarely in the eye, in ourselves and in the world, that we begin to at least see the light. And that is the alchemy of personal transformation. In the midst of the deepest, darkest night, when we feel most humbled by life, the faint shadow of our wings begins to appear. Only when we have faced the limits of what we can do, does the limitlessness of what God can do begin to dawn on us. It is the depth of the darkness now confronting our world that will reveal to us the magic of who we truly are. We are spirit, and thus, we are more than the world. When we remember that, the world itself will bow to our remembrance.

Marianne Williamson, from *A Year of Miracles*

✤ REMEMBER ✤

Together, let's take a deep breath, hold up a
welcome sign for transformation and grab
courage by the horns to say, bring it on!
The journey it takes will be worth the
evolution in your soul.

CHAPTER 8

Saved by the Practice

SOMETHING OCCURRED many years ago that changed my life. I am forever grateful for it, and so grateful for the wonderful woman that brought it to be. I don't know that she even remembers the power of what she taught me, but it was definitely life-changing for me on my path. Often the person that has changed our life by something they did or said doesn't even remember doing it. It's a clear sign that when Spirit wants us to know something, we will get the message one way or another, even if the messenger does not remember delivering the blessings. So, this was mine.

Years ago, when I was studying to be a licensed spiritual practitioner, I began seeing my own practitioner as I was very interested in healing different issues of my own. To this day I believe it is vitally important to stay accountable when working in the healing field, to keep up on self-care and have consistent check-in sessions with our own practitioner or therapist. It keeps us clean and available to our clients.

As a student, I would go to see my practitioner regularly, and a pattern became very evident. Each time I would sit with her, I would proceed to reel off story after story of all that was occurring in my life. The challenges that were overwhelming, the frustrations, the confusion, all of it came tumbling out in our sessions like a waterfall of unending issues, and they were all very dramatic! I observed my wonderful practitioner doing what she did best, which was knowing the Truth for me even in the midst of all my stories.

When I would finally take a breath in between expressing all of the catastrophes, she would gently take a breath as well, and ask me this question, "Kimberly, tell me, what has your practice been like this week? What have you been willing to practice in the midst of all of this?" Well, with this question I would not even hesitate to interrupt her because I was usually on quite a roll. I would quickly react with some version of the following: "Oh, well I had absolutely NO time to meditate, it was too crazy, and I can't even find my journal to do any writing. But, let me tell you what else happened to me." And at that moment I would passionately jump into another very dramatic version of something that happened to me that I wanted her to fix! I was sure she had the key to fixing all of it. Why else was I coming to see her? She was AMAZING.

I knew I had the very best practitioner ever, so whatever I was dealing with, she was sure to advise me, this I KNEW. But what I did not know was that she had no intention at all to "fix"me. She was clear I did not need fixing.

So, week after week, session after session this same thing would occur. I would share all the crap that was going on in my life, and she would ask the same question, "Kimberly, what has your practice been like this week?"

I GOT THE WAKE-UP CALL!

Until one day it all changed. Yes, the miracle came. I finally woke up and heard her! Oh my, I actually heard what she was asking me, and I got the insight. On that day, I answered in this way: "Okay, I finally get it, you are going to keep asking me that same question over and over again until I finally stop giving you excuses and begin to practice what I know I need to practice."

Gently, and without any judgment whatsoever, she nodded her head and said, yes. She knew all along what I could not see. That the situations in my life were never going to change until I changed how I was dealing with them. Better yet, until I changed my patterns and began practicing my spiritual practice.

Here is the thing, we can continue to talk about it, and continue to talk about doing it, but until we actually put into motion what we speak of, then it's just theory, not practice.

That which transforms your life is what you practice. And what you practice constitutes your personal laws of life — not what you merely believe in, but what you practice! Rudimentary spirituality is theory; advanced spirituality is practice!

Michael Bernard Beckwith

To talk about one thing but not live it is against everything I stand for and teach. At the beginning of my journey, I did not realize this is what I was doing, but thank goodness for someone who loved me so much that she did not judge me; she just stood vigil for me to wake up to my inner knowing and grow. For this, I am forever grateful.

Looking out into the world, we can see that there are certain individuals that live by this. Any athlete that makes it to the heights of success without a doubt knows that it was due to their consistency in their practice. There is an understanding that athletes must practice becoming talented, strong and proficient at their chosen sport. They do not hesitate just because it's a day that they don't feel like exercising. What they feel like doesn't really matter to them, as it is more about what they are committed to. Our commitments guide our direction, and what truly drives us is a high vision and our passion to fulfill it.

INNER STRENGTH

Too often, when it comes to building inner strength, or spiritual muscle, our humanness tries to convince us that we can do it tomorrow. We all know it takes a commitment to live our practice, and yet we resist.

Meditation takes commitment each day, to set the alarm 30 or 60 minutes before the rest of the house begins the day. It calls for a commitment to keeping an ongoing intention practice each moment, but it will change your life. It takes self-love and a strong desire to evolve and stay committed to daily practices that grow us, that expand us. It has been proven to be effective and powerfully rewarding. If I could be given a dime for every time a client said to me, "But it is so hard, Kim," ah, I would be a very wealthy woman. (And by the way, in my definition of wealthy, I am already there! More on that later.)

But let's get real, "it" being hard has nothing to do with it. Not one thing. What I say to many is, "Do you want to continue to fight for your limitations, for how hard it is, or do you want to be free?" I did not sign up to keep you small and agree to any of your self-imposed limitations. I signed up to help you wake up and live your life fully present! And what I KNOW is that it is the practice and your commitment to stay in practice that will save your life!

YOUR PRACTICE

There is a special quote I think I have read out loud to masses of people over a thousand times. It is one I live by and ask my clients to embody.

What we practice, we ultimately embody; what we practice, we become. It is that simple.

Our practice is as individual as each of us. I define spiritual practice as that which connects us to Source, God, Spirit, the Universe and the practice is to stay connected with every breath you take.

You are the thinker.
You are the creator of thought patterns.
You are the master of your fate.
But you must exercise this mastership.

Ernest Holmes, *This Thing Called You*

For some people, their spiritual practice might include any or all of the practices on this list:

Prayer

Intention setting

Meditation

Journaling

Gratitude and Acknowledgment writing

Visioning

Chanting

Yoga

Walking meditation

Hiking in nature

Forgiveness

Worship services

Tithing

Inspirational reading

Classes on personal transformation

TRANSFORMATIONAL BREATH WORK

One of my clients is a proficient surfer, and his daily practice is to get to the ocean, paddle out, take a deep breath and meditate alone on his board, connecting with Source. Each of us must honor our individuality and ponder what connects us to the divine. I invite you now to consider what honors you and write your own list of practices that you will put into place and begin today:

1._____

2._____

3._____

4._____

5._____

It requires an embodiment of discipline to keep your practice alive and active. It is not something for the weak of heart. Life is not to be viewed as a passerby; it is to be fully embodied. Your practice will become a level of devotion, devotion to your life! To yourself! You become devoted to your own evolution, and to this precious incarnation, this existence.

Are you ready and willing to live to the fullness of your life? What are you willing to give, to commit to on a moment-by-moment basis? I am willing to give my life to have my life in this precious incarnation. To give my life, I am committed to my daily practice, for it has saved my life and I will never forget it.

Spiritual practice is not just sitting and meditating. Practice is looking, thinking, touching, drinking, eating and talking. Every act, every breath, and every step can be practice and can help us to become more ourselves.

Thich Nhat Hanh

Many people tell me that they do fine and well living their practice until something big comes up and interrupts the time they had committed to it. It can be a job change, a death in the family, a birth in the family, the breakup of a relationship. The list is endless. My response to them is, that is precisely when your practice lifts you the most! You must practice right through the center of whatever dilemma crosses your path!

Your practice is your fuel, your practice is your fire, and your practice gets you through the storm. Recently, when a disaster occurred in my beautiful community, a client came to me and asked, "How can you still live a life of intention and believe in prayer now? How can you keep praying?" I looked at him with the fullness of my love for all I believe in and said,

> "This is no time to doubt Spirit. This is when I lean in even more! I set my intentions and pray even more, and I KNOW with unstoppable faith that they are being heard!"

The prayers I speak are not beseeching words, but instead affirmative language that connects me to source, to the truth of who I am and places me in alignment with the unlimited nature of Spirit. I refuse to abandon my practice in the midst of the storm, and I invite you to do the same!

> You practice your practice until your life is your practice!

PRACTICE IN MOTION

My own personal practice is never stagnant. It is always evolving and growing. I lean into it when the winds get rough and I have learned to practice in motion. What I mean by this is, when the storms are heavy, when you get an emergency call from the hospital, or you come upon someone in trouble, you do not stop and say you will practice when you get home to your meditation pillow. You do it right where you are! You begin in the midst of the challenge and you keep practicing right through it.

The practice, your own personal toolbox, is what gets you through the journey of life! I have been known to start meetings in legal mediations with an out-loud intention before the meeting, to pray in the hallways of courtrooms, to meditate in the waiting room of hospitals. Wherever we may be, there is always room to live our practice!

In the midst of writing this book, I had the opportunity to put my practice into high gear. (There are no accidents. I got to live what I know in the middle of writing all about it.) It again became urgently necessary for me to apply what I am expressing to you, the power of fearlessly putting my practice into motion. Life gave me a very big opportunity to do just that, and truly, the gratitude I have for having these tools is indescribable.

It was a November afternoon when I opened my office door to say goodbye to a client and immediately noticed the smell in the air. It was clear that fire was near. When you live in the Malibu mountains long enough you become sensitive to the time of the year when the Santa Ana winds are blowing, and to the heightened awareness of the fire dangers while these winds are having their way. It was that day; a fire was near.

I said goodbye to my client and called my local fire captain, who I have come to know over the years. He confirmed, yes indeed, there was not only one fire in motion, but two. One was in the north, and the other one was quite a distance away in the valley. He just reminded me that I knew the drill, and even though it seemed far away, to always be prepared. I took a big deep breath and set a bold intention.

My intention is to stay calm and centered as I make conscious choices and prepare my family for all that is before us.

Within the hour calls started coming in. My very dear friend Michelle, who used to work with the Red Cross and was still on all the high-alert notices, called and asked me to leave the house immediately. I lovingly thanked her but reminded her that the location of the fire was in Bell Canyon, and as she used to live there, we were both acutely aware of the distance and that the fire was over 25 miles away from me. I felt it was not near at that point and I did not need to evacuate yet. She was firm and kept her request strong, and as the night wore on, she began to get even more vocal in her pleading for me to get out. I repeated my intention, stayed calm and promised my friends I would have the important paper file ready to go at the door if I needed to leave quickly.

At this point I knew being alone at home with my two bullmastiff dogs, there was no room in my car for anything else for me to take with me. If we had to run, the dogs and I, with a bunny on the front seat, we would evacuate when need be. I stayed in prayer and powerful intention as the night got darker and smoke filled the air.

At 10 in the evening, my daughter, Lila, unexpectedly came home with her boyfriend, Andrew, who had been evacuated from his college dorm. Unbeknown to us at the time, it would turn out to be an amazing blessing that they were with me at the house. The three of us watched the news and decided that we would make a decision in the morning. In those late hours, it was clear that the fire was still quite a distance away, or so it seemed. We all went to sleep a little after midnight.

Only two and a half hours later, Lila came into my bedroom to wake me up. She was trying to stay calm, but I could see the fear in her eyes. She said, "Mom, our phones are blowing up with alerts, the fire has jumped the freeway, and they have just evacuated Westlake. I think we need to go now!" I took a deep breath, listened to her and was grateful that she woke me. Oddly enough, my phone NEVER received the alerts. If Lila and Andrew were not there that night, the fire would have made it to my door before I ever saw it coming. The first miracle indeed!

We began the process of evacuating. I asked Lila to stay as calm as possible and we repeated the intention again.

My intention is to stay calm and centered as I make conscious choices and prepare my family for all that is before us.

I reminded her we did not need to run, the fire was still a bit away, just not much. Although Westlake is our neighbor and the people of that community were being evacuated, the fire was not there yet, but it was on its way.

The winds were still crazy intense and as the fire jumped the 101 freeway, the warnings were that it was not going to stop until it hit the ocean. We were located smack in the middle of that path to the ocean. The danger was beyond evident.

Since Andrew had a larger vehicle than mine, I began handing him some important items. My computers first (the book was on there), then just a couple of large pictures on the wall, and one tub of photo albums. For some reason, I could not find the rest of my treasured photo albums. Lila put her bunny in a travel box and added him along with one bag of her clothes. In a bit of a daze I attempted to pack a bag but did not know what to take. As the bag needed to be small enough to fit on my front seat, I only packed a pair of jeans, tennis shoes, a few pairs of undergarments and one or two T-shirts. I truly felt I would be coming home to all my belongings and did not need to panic and take everything with me. We had been through this drill before and always made it safely. This time it felt more intense, but I still did not think there was a chance that my beloved home and beautiful sanctuary would be reduced to ashes.

In the dark, I sensed Lila getting nervous; she wanted to get going. I told the two of them to go ahead as I wanted to walk through the house one more time before heading out. She began to cry and said she could not leave without me, but I reminded her that I would move quickly, be right behind them and would call as soon as I was on Pacific Coast Highway. We hugged and she and Andrew and the bunny left.

Alone in the dark, the dogs already in the car, I walked back into my home. I realized I had forgotten my contact lenses. Thank goodness I remembered. As I went to get them, I slowly began to look around. I felt the need to bless my beautiful home, and all we had built there. I began by blessing my bedroom, my bathroom and then the library, the living room and kitchen. It was important for me to appreciate and honor each room and say a prayer for safety. Lastly, I walked into my office and suddenly looked up at my overflowing bookcase. I had quite an enormous collection of brilliant books that I had gathered and treasured over the years.

In dedicating my life to study, my collection of powerful wisdom in the form of files of notes, cases of books and audio learning was massive. As I looked at the bookcase in my office, I asked myself, what books could I not live without if something DID happen? Immediately my eyes landed on my two favorites and I reached up and grabbed them both. *Spiritual Liberation* by Michael Bernard Beckwith and *This Thing Called You* by Ernest Holmes. They were treasures packed with years and years of notes.

As I reached for them, I suddenly noticed something beautiful. The shelf above them was the place where all of my journals were lined up. I smiled seeing the unlimited amounts of information I had collected from insights, thoughts, inspirational input from great spiritual leaders, as well as the journals I had written to my children when they were little. It was as if they were all presented on that shelf asking me to take them. By the grace of God, I reached high, grabbed them all and put them in the last bag as I headed out the door. I squeezed the bag onto the floorboard, told my dogs we would be okay, looked back at my home in the dark, and slowly pulled away. That was the last time I saw my treasured and beloved sanctuary.

I drove to my parents in the dark, repeating my intention over and over, and arrived around five in the morning. For 24 hours we sat glued to the TV, turning it off only to sleep. Watching the destruction, looking for signs if it was near my neighborhood, watching friends get the news that their homes were taken by the power of the firestorm. It was all too much to believe. Our community was ablaze and there did not seem to be an end in sight. I cried myself to sleep thinking of the loss my dear friends must be feeling.

The next morning the call came from a very dear friend. Through his own tears, he delivered the news, my home was gone as well. It was all gone, the retreat center, office, home, horse barn (which was empty, thank goodness) . . . everything had burned to the ground.

The fire had swallowed it up as it was heading to the ocean. I was later told that over 50% of the structures in my neighborhood had been destroyed. Our community did not have a chance against Mother Nature and the fury of that wind-and-fire explosion. Everything in its path was taken. The wrath of Mother Nature had scooped up my life and left ashes in its wake.

I prayed a lot that day; through the tears I prayed. I was grateful for so much. Grateful Lila had come home that night, grateful I had a bed to sleep in at my parents for the moment, grateful for all the assistance that began to flow in, grateful my mom was holding me as the sobs came flowing outward. As the shock began to lighten, the awareness of how much I was loved and supported began to be felt at my core.

PRACTICE AT WORK

The practices of prayer, intention, gratitude, journaling, open receptivity, accepting support from my community, it all saved me. Without it, I would have drowned in tears and been stuck in the "Why did this happen to me?" That question would not have served me at all. I needed every bit of strength and clarity to focus on the decisions that had to be made moment-by-moment.

When different people would say to me, "How are you doing okay through all of this, Kim? You just lost everything!" My answer was the same. . . my practice, my faith and my willingness to accept help from others were what was carrying me through.

When I did make it back to the property weeks later, to my amazement, only one thing was left standing. As if rising from the ash, my sacred statue of the goddess Quan Yin was still erect right outside my office door, as if she was greeting me. Quan Yin is the goddess of compassion and mercy and I was acutely aware of her message. It was a miracle and definitely answered prayer. She still stood. Surrounded by ash, she stood tall. Nothing left but her. Answered prayer at its finest.

Your practice will save your life. Mine has over and over again, and I am beyond grateful for it!

Our practice, our toolbox is not created just to be filled with wisdom and then to be placed on a shelf. It is to be embodied, used and used again and again.

Nonstop wisdom is to be lived. It is a human mistake to think that just because one has read a lot, studied for years, been in the presence of great spiritual masters, that they are embodying the knowledge. True embodiment takes practice, repeated and lived practice! We must choose to live it in motion, not just know it as information. Mastery is to live what we know!

The difference between knowledge and wisdom is, knowledge is something you know, but wisdom is something you LIVE!

The key is our willingness to not abandon our toolbox when the road gets rough. Our tools must go into overdrive when the road gets rough and it is only by our conscious choice to stay in practice in the storm that this can happen.

It is so important to know that our well-practiced and disciplined mind will automatically lean into Spirit when the road gets tough. It becomes an automatic response once it has been fully practiced, activated and lived! We must stay alert, take a breath to let the emotion of the moment wash over us and grab a tool and activate it. With every breath, we can choose again to rise up after we stumble or fall!

My intention is to be unshakable and stand strong in faith as I move through all that is before me!

Moment by moment, breath by breath, choice by choice we get there. Living bold intentions with every breath and every choice in life leads us to powerful actions. We are guided to make wise decisions, as our decisions follow the powerful intentions that are well practiced and fine-tuned! The clarity of our intentions opens the door for Spirit to support us in more expansive ways than we can humanly imagine. Our commitment is to stay on the path, regardless if it feels hard or easy. We must stay on the path. Instead of getting caught up and knocked over by our day-to-day issues, let us aways remember the depth of this power that is always available and only a thought away. It is our power of choice to implement intentions—through the good times as well as the dark moments—that lift us to high levels of transformation.

> *Prayer reweaves the rent fabric of the universe.*
> *It releases us, in time, from the snares of lower*
> *energies . . . Prayer and meditation reconnect*
> *us with our Source.*
>
> Marianne Williamson

To consciously create your life, it is necessary to put a clear practice into place. If not, your life will just happen by happenstance, and you will be creating unconsciously. But, if you wish to create your life consciously, spiritual practice is absolutely necessary. You choose your practice, and my strong request is that you begin it NOW! If you already have an active practice, then expand it now! It is an evolving thing, and I invite you to keep it alive, so it keeps you alive!

ᓚ **REMEMBER** ᓚ

Take a deep breath and forever embrace a bold intention to be present to all that is going on in the world, yet not be shaken by it. We are in the world, yet we are not of the world.

CHAPTER 9

Conscious Creation: Name It, Claim It, Create It

STAYING CONSCIOUS is the most important job we have right now. I am not just referring to staying "awake" in our bodies, although I am pointing to staying conscious in our awakened bodies. We are always responsible for our life experience, and the moment-by-moment choices we make define what those experiences will be. Staying conscious in our choices and the decisions we make is crucial.

We are creators, and with every breath, we are engaging in the creation of our life experience. Our choices propel power into motion, and if we are not conscious of what we choose, then we are creating by default. The law of cause and effect does not take a day off. The Universe is always with us, responding to our thoughts, wishes and the practices we have in place. It is the divine teacher of responding. Let us be divine students and be willing to stay alert and aware in all that we create.

It is our responsibility to stay alert to where our thoughts are leading us. Are your thoughts filled with abundance, forgiveness, joy and success? Or are you creating more of something you no longer desire?

You can choose to stay awake and create from your heart, and to create all that you wish to experience. You can clean up your thinking by consistently using the tools in your spiritual toolbox. At any moment that you catch your chatter taking you down a path of destruction and judgment, you can take a breath, and make a choice to stand in the light and fullness of who you are and consciously choose again! Choose success, choose joy and choose abundance; choose love, choose forgiveness, choose YOU!

No matter what may appear before you, even if it seems to be in the appearance of the opposite of this, see through it and choose what you desire to experience. The Universe is listening, so take responsibility for what you think and what you choose! The mind chatter that is inaccurate and does not support you doesn't have to take up space any longer unless you let it. Take a breath and choose again!

My intention is to assist you to stay conscious. To assist you to create the life you wish for and to do it intentionally. You have the tools, now you get to live them. I have been told that when my clients first start to write intentions, the words do not always come through so easily. So, I am offering up a couple of pages to assist you on your path of beginning to live an intentional life. I have broken them down into different areas of your life to be more helpful. You can use these or alter them to fit your own needs more accurately. Enjoy!

BODY TEMPLE:

My intention is to make choices today that are loving to myself and to my body.

My intention today is to stretch my body in new ways and experience more strength and flexibility.

My intention is to love my body through all of its changes.

My intention is to stand tall in my acts of self-love as I continue to make choices of divine health and healing.

My intention is to be grateful for this body that I have and nurture it with self-care.

My intention is to remember I am bigger than any apparent diagnosis.

My intention is to accept that I am the space where healing is taking place, and every cell of my body temple is in divine wholeness.

LOVE:

My intention is to remember who I am.

My intention is to love myself completely and with an open heart of acceptance!

My intention is to be loving in my actions, my thoughts and my choices.

My intention is to love myself this day and always, through every step of this precious journey.

My intention is to give and receive my love freely today.

My intention is to be open to random acts of kindness to myself as I stay willing to love myself more deeply.

My intention is to live a life of unwavering faith and walk boldly in creating an intentional life of unlimited joy and happiness.

RELATIONSHIP:

My intention is to remember that in every relationship there is room for all to be honored, loved and respected.

My intention is to open my heart and speak words of loving kindness to all I encounter this day.

My intention is to accept the most loving relationship that honors me as I honor my beloved.

My intention is to nurture the relationships in my life with gentleness and compassion.

My intention is to embrace my family with love and acceptance!

My intention is to allow others to assist me along my path.

My intention is to speak from my heart with kindness, love and respect.

BUSINESS:

My intention is to create the life I dream of by making choices that are in alignment with my highest good.

My intention is to accept unlimited success and joy in all my endeavors.

My intention is to stay centered, empowered and clear in all of my business ventures.

My intention is to call forth and accept unlimited assistance as I achieve all of my dreams and goals.

My intention is to easily and effortlessly complete the tasks before me that lift my business to new heights of success.

My intention is to stand in my power, courageously release my past and accept unlimited success.

FINANCES:

My intention is to see the truth through any appearance of lack and remember that I live in an abundant Universe.

My intention is to call forth and accept unlimited financial freedom and joy.

My intention is to know all my needs are met even before I ask.

My intention is to practice the law of circulation and trust that it is always in motion in my life.

My intention is to remember that abundance comes to me as I trust and circulate my abundance, knowing there is always more than enough.

My intention is to be a good steward of my finances!

My intention is to open wide the availability in my heart to receive unlimited financial abundance.

OVERALL IMPORTANT INTENTIONS:

My intention is to live a life of powerful gratitude with every step I take.

My intention is to release the doing and live in the present moment.

My intention is to stay connected to Source as I move through my day.

My intention is to stay awake, aware and conscious in all my interactions as I move through this beautiful life experience.

I invite you to take these intentions and bring them to life. Let them inspire you, guide you and support you as you embody your spiritual practice! They are not to be left on the page, they are to be lived. By YOU! Do whatever you need to get these intentions before you daily. Repeat them when you rise, repeat them before you walk into your workday, repeat them as you pick up the phone to have a conversation with another, and repeat them often. They are your ticket to transformation! Use these as your samples until you write your own, so that you consciously choose to create what you desire!

Your greatest life is not based on circumstances, your greatest life is based on consciousness!

Staying conscious is our priority now. Conscious choices empower us, conscious choices keep us out of reaction and into responding to each situation before us. When we are responding versus reacting, we have more power in the present moment to choose wisely. Our wisdom is needed!

The world is changing rapidly, calling out to us for a bold wake-up. Each one of us has a choice in how we are going to participate in these changes. I believe as spiritual beings it is our charge to stay awake and aware so that we are contributing to an awakened society. As the world changes, it does not behoove us to sleep through these changes pretending not to take responsibility. We must stay alert, conscious and respond in love.

∽ REMEMBER ∽

Let's take a deep breath and understand the importance of staying empowered and awake. This is the way we can move through the changes with grace and strength. The future evolution of our planet is depending on us!

CHAPTER 10

Clarity Is Power

OUR WORDS ARE ENERGY, and always creating. If we wish to create all that we desire, we must be CLEAR on what we are asking for. It is necessary that our intentions be fueled with crystal-clear language. Clarity propels action into motion. Clarity is power!

We infuse power into the creative process for all of our manifestations to unfold with ease and effortlessness when we are clear! The powerful infusion of crystal-clear clarity creates unbridled energy to bring forth unparalleled manifestation in overflow. That is what we are aiming for, an ongoing receptivity to fulfilled manifestations!

Spirit is always responding to us, and the clearer we are, the more direct the response we receive back. When we are not clear, we run amok in confusion and then we wonder why we only experience more of the same. Frustration seeps in as it seems we just continue to create manifestations we do not want. This is the importance of our practice!

As we continue to stay on top of observing where our thoughts are, then we have the power to consciously choose the words that best support our desires. If there are thoughts that no longer serve us, then we can choose to lovingly release and let go of them, even if they may have been deeply seated within our consciousness. Our job is to set the intention to stay aware of our language and to courageously catch and release any language patterns that keep us limited. The clearer you are, the more you open the portal for Spirit to deliver all your desires fulfilled!

> My intention is to courageously observe my thoughts
> and cultivate the foundation for all I desire to manifest
> with ease.

CLEAR THINKING

The Three Power Pillars keep us in the present, basing our language on qualities, not outcomes. When we live with the three-step process of writing intentions, clarity will come naturally. As you live a life of intention you will continually gain insights into how powerful and necessary clear thinking is! Let me share with you a perfectly clear example.

When I first began my path of spiritual awakening, I received a very strong lesson in manifestation that taught me the importance of clarity. It is a lesson that was painful to experience. However, I got the message and never forgot it. I had direct experience with the importance and the power of clarity as a necessity in my intentions!

I was out of college in my early twenties and had been modeling and acting for a few years. I felt alive in the process of acting and was committed to continuing to grow and succeed at it. As I had just begun discovering the power of intentions, I was excited to create one that was aimed at succeeding in the field I was so enmeshed in. At that time, I lived in the San Francisco area and my acting jobs were consistent but small in size, based on what was being filmed in the area. I knew I needed to move to Los Angeles. My first step, of course, was to create an intention to get me to Southern California. So, here is what I created:

My intention is to land a national commercial that gets me my SAG union card so I can move to Los Angeles.

(Note, as I was new to this, you can see where the Three Power Pillars were not completely being used here. I was aiming at an outcome, and more in the future than the present moment!)

In the business of acting, to move forward one must have their Screen Actors Guild card. I did not have mine and was determined that I needed it before I moved to Los Angeles. I was not leaving the comfort of my stomping ground, where

I felt like I was a big fish in a little pond, to move to the huge pond as a tadpole and try to get work without being in the union. I was clear about that! So, I set my intention and focused on it daily.

Within a very short time I booked a national commercial for Toyota scooters. I was ecstatic and beyond grateful. The Universe heard me. I got my national commercial, which would get me my union card. Fulfilled intention for sure! I was feeling unstoppable and ready to head to Southern California!

After shooting the commercial, I began preparing my move. I gave notice to my roommate, alerted my family and started making plans to gather up my personal belongings, prepare things for my dog, my horse, and head south! Within a month or two, I had rented a truck and trailer, loaded up my two best friends (Tasha the Doberman pinscher and Rascal the quarter horse) and headed down the road. I chuckle now at the thought of how wild this must have appeared.

It was a stormy rainy day, and there I was, a young woman towing a horse trailer down the state of California with a guard dog sitting passenger! I arrived during the night, got everyone safely where they needed to be, took a breath and slept with a grateful heart. The next chapter of life was taking off and I could not have been more excited.

Yet, a turn of events happened quite quickly. To my surprise and disbelief, only days later I got a call from my agent in San Francisco.

"Kim, are you sitting down? I hate to tell you this but [this intro never has a good ending] we were just informed by the production company that your scene has hit the editing room floor. You will not be in the final cut of the commercial, which means you will not make any residual money from your national commercial. We are so sorry to have to bring you this news!"

Now, initially, I was stunned and overwhelmingly upset. I had just moved to a new town, left behind all I knew and was beginning my career. I was expecting (keyword) that I would have my residual payments as the financial base to support me until I got myself established. In the acting world, residual checks are a wonderful way to make sure all the bills are paid while auditioning for other jobs. So, with this news, it was very clear that was not going to happen for me. I felt like someone had kicked me in the gut. After releasing a lot of tears and doing all I could to keep fear at bay, I began to make a new plan for my financial stability and still move forward in creating a life in Los Angeles.

It was not until years later that I got crystal-clear clarity on what had happened and where I had set myself up for this fall. This is often the case when hardship comes, and the challenges are intense; we cannot initially comprehend why things are falling apart.

We must lean into faith and keep moving forward when the walls are coming down, only to later fully understand what was being established or released. When I looked at my intention, it was CLEAR in the wording, that I got EXACTLY what I had asked for! I got a national commercial, which is what I asked for, and I got into the union, which is also what I asked for! But I did NOT ask to land a powerful national commercial and receive the financial blessings that would come from that! That was my expectation! So even in this intention, unbeknown to me, there were some inklings of expectation in my wording!

I wanted a union card, as I saw that as my ticket to L.A., and I got just that! No more, no less, just exactly what I had put into my intention. Clarity is power! Even if it is hard to look at sometimes, the most challenging moments can bring us a deeper understanding of what is necessary for our own inner growth. This big challenge, hitting the editing room floor and not making it to the final cut of "my" national commercial, taught me something I never forgot!

From that moment onward, I was led by the awareness of how important it is to have crystal-clear clarity and to put into words the true desire of what I wished to manifest. With what I know now, my intention may have looked like this:

My intention is to call forth a clear pathway to receiving
my SAG union card, and to accept the abundance of
acting opportunities along the way.

There is a direct connection between clear intentions and powerful manifestation. As the energetic field of creation is always listening and the law of cause and effect does not take a day off, it is evident that manifestations are always unfolding. Let us be conscious of all that we are creating and stay awake in remembering the ability we have to use our words wisely. Our job is to focus on the qualities of what we desire and to aim them in the direction of what we wish to create. The rest is up to the Universe.

THE COURAGE TO MOVE FORWARD

Now, there is an additional step of clarity that I would like to discuss here. Sometimes, when the path before us is very confusing and we do not know which way to turn, the need for clarity becomes the intention.

My intention is to call forth divine clarity and guidance
for all that is before me in my life.

When we are at a crossroads and are unsure which direction to go, it is necessary to ask for divine assistance on the best choice before us. There are moments when the confusion is overwhelming, the choices before us are expansive and there is an awareness that whatever decisions we make may profoundly impact our lives and the lives of others. Whether it be that we seek clarity in a relationship, a job, a possible move, a health issue, whatever it may be, often the only intention we may utter is FOR clarity. Knowing that the Universe always listens and responds, we can rest assured that our intention for clarity will be answered.

What we may not know at those moments is that as we begin to more fully trust the presence to guide us, to bring us the fulfilled intention, there is also a chance that the clarity we asked for may be more than we wanted or were prepared to handle when it comes.

Sometimes the clarity is to move in a direction we fear, or to leave a relationship that does not honor us, or to embark upon a new job adventure. The bottom line is, the clarity we receive may scare us. It will still be fulfilled intention, yet it may create within us a panic on some level. For this reason, I suggest that when we ask for clarity in our intentions, we also ask for something else that is vitally important and must go hand in hand with clarity.

What I am speaking of is COURAGE. The courage to move forward on the clarity that comes! We may need a lot of courage to fulfill the direction that the clarity gives us.

My intention is to call forth divine guidance and crystal-clear clarity on my relationship, and for the courage to move forward with strength.

Courage is vitally important on any path of self-growth. The road is not always easy, and to grow involves growing pains. We must constantly be stretching our mind, listening expansively and staying willing to trust Spirit. So, our courageous spirit is a necessary element upon the path. The lion in *The Wizard of Oz* knew this, and this is why he wanted it so badly. Courage infuses momentum and creates a sense of power that can move mountains. Courage is the light within your soul that was sparked into being with your very first breath. Stand now and set bold intentions that have crystal-clear clarity!

> *Life shrinks or expands in proportion*
> *to one's courage.*
>
> Anaïs Nin

We have the ability and blessing to create our world. YOU now have the key to create consciously the world you want. So, what do you *wish* to speak into expression? Remember you have a choice, you have the power to create, and you have the gift of thought and language to propel your intentions forward. All that is required is within you. And the power resides in your choice, so . . . be clear and go forth and create the life of your dreams. Clarity is POWER!

∽ **REMEMBER** ∽

Take a deep breath and set your intentions boldly and clearly with confidence.
Call forth powerful courage and fulfill all that you desire!

CHAPTER 11

Gratitude, Celebration, Acknowledgment

The Foundation of Receiving

THERE ARE THREE MORE very powerful and important practices that cannot be missed along the path of intentional living. They comprise a valuable team in creating an awakened life, and it is imperative to begin to allow these three to be activated for unlimited fulfillment of your intentions. These three powerhouses are GRATITUDE, CELEBRATION and ACKNOWLEDGMENT! Without these elements fully practiced, we can jeopardize our ability to continue to manifest all we are intending. These simple practices create a foundation of receptivity that will allow you to accept more good than you have ever imagined!

As we express our gratitude, we must never forget that the highest appreciation is not to utter words, but to live by them.

John F. Kennedy

GRATITUDE

Let's begin with gratitude first. Always a good place to start. John F. Kennedy said it so well, stating that the highest appreciation is to live by gratitude, not just utter the words. To live with a grateful heart is to appreciate all that comes before us, the blessings as well as the challenges. As we cultivate a life of deep appreciation, the burdens that come before us will begin to shift, and we will open up to experiencing them as expansive blessings. Every blessing is an opportunity to stand more firmly in gratitude, and every utterance of appreciation brings more blessings!

Living a life of gratitude enables you to receive more than you ever thought possible. Gratitude is one of the cornerstones of living a life of unlimited happiness and awakened joy. If it is true that what we focus on expands, and it is, then it is simple to comprehend that when you focus on gratitude, you will be given more to be grateful for. It is one of the oldest spiritual laws and one that is profoundly important. Lives change when one is grateful! We change when we are activating a grateful heart!

Being in gratitude heightens our awareness of where things are working well. We are focused on all that is good, all that is occurring in perfect order, and all that is being delivered to us with grace and ease. We are expanding our consciousness, not restricting it. As we are energetic beings, the resonance of gratitude builds our energetic field and keeps us open and receptive. Those that are grateful are aware that the Universe is always bringing more, and giving thanks builds the foundation for more good to happen. A grateful heart paves the way for an abundance of good to come rushing in, even when we don't expect it. Hear me clearly, please: we have the ability to alter the direction of our lives by altering the depth of what we are grateful for.

Being spiritual has nothing to do with what you believe and everything to do with your state of consciousness.

Eckhart Tolle

Each day we get to be appreciative of the very blessing of being alive, for being able to take our next breath. Just the opportunity we have to remember that we have a body and we are present in this existence, this alone is so much more than enough to be grateful for. We can do so much, we can be so much; the possibilities are endless. There is always good waiting for us, yet we are oblivious to it if we are not living in a space of gratitude for all that we already have. Living in a state of appreciation is a powerful place to be in creating the life we desire.

Here is a tool and an invitation to you. A practice that keeps us in alignment with truly seeing all we are grateful for and embodying it, is to begin writing a gratitude journal. It is easy, and looks like this:

Date:
Today, I am grateful for:

1._____

2._____

3._____

4._____

5._____

Go ahead, you can write it now, this is your book and if not, whoever owns the book will probably smile when they see what you are grateful for. I suggest my clients keep a gratitude journal and write in it daily. I find that writing at the end of the day, before bed, is a beautiful exercise. At that time, it is so important to reflect back on all that occurred during the day that you are grateful for. A gratitude journal is guaranteed to change your sleep patterns and definitely assists in creating a calm consciousness when you awaken in the morning. I personally keep my gratitude journal on my bathroom counter so that I write in it right before bedtime. I don't miss it, as it is sitting right there near my toothbrush! It only takes a moment or two, and the last thoughts that you take to the pillow are all that you appreciate. Imagine that, it can put a smile on your face just considering it. Imagine what it does for your cells and muscles as you close your eyes.

Gratitude makes sense of our past, brings peace for today and creates a vision for tomorrow.

Melodie Beattie

Years ago, one of my clients experienced an unforeseen beautiful gift that came from writing in her daily gratitude journal. At my annual intention retreat, I invited everyone to take on the practice to write in their gratitude journals every day for an entire year. Well, this client took that on with a lot of commitment. She wrote in her gratitude journal every night before bed without missing even one day.

Toward the end of the year, one night her husband came to bed to join her and he gently asked her, "Honey, could you tell me about that book in the bathroom? It has so many beautiful things about me in it and I do not know what it is." Talk about a happy moment in that marriage! So often she had written about gratitude and appreciation for her life and her husband, and he received the blessings of it.

Her intention was to keep her commitment to write daily and stay in strong gratitude. By doing that one thing, she shifted something huge in her marriage. Can you see how the benefits of writing about gratitude expands beyond anything you can imagine? It literally changes the vibration of your reality! Everything is different through the eyes of appreciation, and all relationships are lifted by it. Ah, the possibilities it creates are endless. The simplest exercises offer up gems in overflow and can create massive change in any area of our lives. One step at a time, one breath at a time, one gratitude at a time, changes everything.

Many clients will tell me, "Oh Kim, I do not write in my gratitude journal, but I repeat the statements in my head." They believe this is good enough, but I beg to disagree.

There is scientific data that shows the power of writing something down versus just thinking about it. When you write statements of gratitude, you remember them, you embody them, you keep them alive and invite more things into your life to be grateful for!

The process of writing things down stimulates our brains and awakens our hearts. The intention is to fully "feel" the things you are grateful for, and then allow your depth of appreciation to drop from your thinking mind to your feeling heart. WRITE IT DOWN!

My intention is to write down all that I am grateful for, as it easily flows from my mind to my heart, via my pen!

I believe the fastest way for us to change the world is to assist our children, our beautiful youth, to discover all that they appreciate in life and all that they are so very grateful for. When this is at the forefront of their consciousness, all else falls into place!

For many years now I have had the blessing to lead retreats for children. It is quite profound to watch the little ones, from five and up, as they sit down and start writing a gratitude journal. I have seen them pause, reflect and reach deep. Some of the things they are grateful for are so simple, and yet others are quite astounding and often surprising. I have also witnessed tears in the eyes of parents as they observe their children expressing all that they are grateful for. Parents share their deep joy and sometimes true surprise, for when these gratitude journals are read aloud, often they had no idea about things their children treasured. Let us speak about gratitude, write down what we are grateful for and continue to see through the eyes of appreciation!

In this fast-moving world, it is necessary for us to create an atmosphere and environment for our children to express themselves. A spacious safety net for them to explore all feelings, thoughts and expressions. For them to know that conversation is acceptable, and communication matters.

Teaching children how to live an intentional life is giving them the tools to create their lives consciously. In a world where they have been raised with visual overload, screens everywhere, tablets that they can tap into with just their finger, it is so very important for them to have tools to stay present. It is necessary and vital for us to create environments that nurture face-to-face conversation, a sharing of what matters, an expression of the soul.

As we make this a priority, the youth of the world will aim to connect and share themselves. All spiritual practices lead us to this path, one of connection, of true oneness. To begin teaching children the power of being grateful, setting intentions and celebrating their magnificence will only lead to a world that honors all, a world of One.

Our charge is to remember it is never too early, and never too late to begin writing what we are grateful for. Appreciation expands our availability to create, so wherever you are, begin it now!

*If the only prayer you said was thank you,
that would suffice.*

Meister Eckhart

CELEBRATION

Now let's look at the practice of celebration!

Over the years I have noticed a very distinct disempowering pattern in many of the clients that come to see me. Something that may seem so small yet is vitally important to catch and interrupt. It is a pattern that can cause havoc in the path of manifestation. It is very necessary to interrupt this pattern so that nothing blocks our channels of accepting all that we desire.

The pattern I am referring to is the one that blocks our ability to pause and truly celebrate the successes and manifestations when they come, no matter how big or small. Most individuals do not know the importance of honoring and celebrating those moments in life when their prayers have been answered! Session after session many clients will quickly sweep over the good that is occurring and completely miss and overlook where all the answered prayers have landed.

We as humans tend to go from problem to problem, fixing one problem and then off to another. We are not usually encouraged to stop and bask for a moment in celebration of what problems were solved. It is a by-product of the speed of all that is occurring in our lives. We as a society have become masterful "fixers," which is commendable, yet I believe it is necessary to pause before the next "fix" begins and reflect for even a single breath. This allows the "fix" to be fully embodied and the recognition of who is doing the fixing to be appreciated.

What I am pointing to looks a lot like this. A client may come in, sit down and jump right into the upset going on in their life. Understandable, this is why they are coming to see me. Yet, often somewhere in their session they take a breath and for a split second begin telling me great things that are occurring, but without a second of hesitation, they then jump right into the very next issue or upset at hand. Not even taking a moment for honoring all the good news. Their focus, their energy is all on what is NOT working! (Remember, I shared in chapter 8 that I did this with my own practitioner!) By jumping right into the very next issue at hand they miss the opportunity to appreciate and celebrate their joyful moment.

You see, usually the good news that is happening in their lives is about all the things we have been praying for during previous sessions. They are all fulfilled intentions. Finally, I firmly stop them in their tracks and say wait, please wait, let's breathe and reflect on what you said about the things that are working in your life. They look at me perplexed as if "Why do I want to talk about that? I have big issues to deal with!" I then explain to them that it is possible that those things that are working, that have shifted, are all things we prayed for weeks and sometimes months ago. I gently ask them to stay conscious with me because by just rolling the success off a list without honoring that they are fully manifested intentions, is not honoring the power that assisted in bringing them forth. They missed a whole level of celebration! There is a missing moment that is too essential to let slip by!

If one does not celebrate and appreciate the manifestation that has been delivered, then one is missing a beautiful opportunity to connect with the Universe in recognition of all it is doing through us. We are not doing this alone!

Once brought to their attention, they often are a bit dismayed that they did not even realize how quickly they were on to the next issue and had not truly given themselves a moment to bask in the place of appreciation for what had occurred. Given awareness, they can choose again.

The Universe is always, always, always (did I say always?) responding to us. It becomes a missed opportunity when we do not notice the power and presence at our fingertips. We are here to say "thank you" to the power within that is responding to us, and the more we recognize it, celebrate it, the more it will deliver miracles at every turn. That is how we cultivate the field of receptivity for more to come to us with ease and effortlessness. By staying in celebration, we create again with the trust and faith that all we are aiming for is coming to us. It always does as we are working with the impersonal law of manifestation!

The more you celebrate your life, the more there is in life to celebrate!

Oprah Winfrey

ACKNOWLEDGMENT

For some, the practice of acknowledgment is the hardest practice to incorporate into their lives. Although it can be challenging, it has been proven that with this one practice, your life will shift to a level of so much abundant good, that you will never again doubt the power of this one thing. The practice I am referring to is writing an acknowledgment journal.

Acknowledgments are similar to gratitude, yet slightly different and have a different impact. Now, the similarity lies in the fact that both keep you very conscious and aware of the good that is occurring in your life. First, the good that you see from looking outside of yourself and seeing all you are appreciative of, and second, the good that you experience that comes from inside, the good you are creating yourself.

The things you are grateful for on your gratitude list do not have to be created by you, but you are very conscious that they're in your life and that they are a blessing to you.

You may be grateful that the sun is shining, grateful to walk barefoot, grateful for the softness of your dogs' ears. All of these things you may be very grateful for, yet you did not make them happen. The difference with acknowledgments is that YOU created the happening, and it could not have occurred without you.

Acknowledgments must be self-involved, self-created or self-motivated. They are created or performed by you. An acknowledgment is an awareness of when we have made a choice or achieved something that we are proud of ourselves for doing. With gratitude we are aware, but we do not have to make any certain thing occur. I noticed that when we see small children achieve things, the adults around them tend to shower the child with a multitude of love, acknowledgment and support. Then as we grow into adults, something else occurs. Somehow, we have accepted a societal belief that to acknowledge ourselves could be egoic.

The intention in writing acknowledgments is in no way an aim to stroke the ego. This is an inner practice to raise the vibration and awareness of where you are growing and making choices that are impactful in shifting the experience of how life unfolds before you. The ego is not getting stroked, the individual is just becoming more awake and aware of the choices they are making. This, in turn, assists us to evolve consciously as we are more aware of our actions and ability to be loving to ourselves as well as to others.

Over the years as I have asked people to write an acknowledgment list as a practice of self-care. I often invite clients to open their journal and on one side of the book write what they are grateful for, and on the other side write what they acknowledge themselves for. I have seen more resistance, hesitation and fear when it comes to acknowledgments. Many individuals who can embody the other exercises with ease stumble on this one. I've saved it for last.

My intention was to build a powerful foundation for you with the other practices so that when you got to acknowledgment it could be one that can be embodied with more ease. When clients and family members in my life struggle with this practice, it very often comes from the inability to see themselves and their brilliance through the eyes of love and acceptance.

This practice is imperative and life-changing, and I ask that you be willing. Think of the small things each day, the moment that you made a choice that was hard or spoke up when it was difficult. Take the time to reflect on who you are, who you are being, and gently begin to write.

Acknowledgments can look something like this:

I acknowledge myself for speaking kindly to my child when I was upset.

I acknowledge myself for taking a breath instead of reacting.

I acknowledge myself for returning that call that I was anxious about today.

I acknowledge myself for completing the tasks on my list.

I acknowledge myself for setting my intentions today.

You get the idea, big or small, write it down! Here, give it a try now.

Date:
Today, I acknowledge myself for:

1._____

2._____

3._____

4._____

5._____

So, how do you feel? I know it might feel awkward to express the things you are doing well, but it is so important. This one practice, the practice of self-acknowledgment, has the power to transform so much in your life!

Acknowledgments do two things, two very important things. The first is that when we write daily acknowledgments, we begin to see ourselves rightly, we begin to see ourselves from the eyes of kindness and love. Very often the judgment voice runs havoc in our minds, and the practice of acknowledgment writing has the power to diminish the judgment voice and bring to the surface the voice of self-love. We expand in love, we shrink in judgment. Our judgment keeps us stuck, our acknowledgment keeps us growing and unfolding. Every self-acknowledgment helps us see ourselves as the Universe sees us; they assist us to see ourselves rightly. Every acknowledgment heals.

The second thing that writing acknowledgments does is prepare your field of receptivity to receive an overflow of more abundant good. Who wouldn't want that? When I speak of the "field of receptivity," here is what I mean. I believe we all have an energetic field that surrounds us. It is an invisible field of consciousness, an energy field that radiates through the space all around our body temples. As we are energetic beings, the energy surrounding us is vibrating and being affected by our thoughts and actions. EVERY acknowledgment infuses love into this field and prepares us to receive more good.

You are adding seeds of good thought to a field of awareness that then vibrates in a manner to receive more good from all pathways. By cultivating this field of receptivity, we invite all of our intentions to be fulfilled. It is a preparation to accept more, to allow more, to say yes to more. The importance of this practice is vital and necessary on our path to living a life of bold intention!

These three gems, GRATITUDE, CELEBRATION and ACKNOWLEDGMENT, are treasures in your toolbox. I invite you to take them out often, practice them with intention and watch the miracles that rise up as your daily existence!

One more thing, don't forget to acknowledge YOU for being YOU, for being willing to grow and evolve. Nobody said it would be easy, but it is definitely worth it!

⌒ REMEMBER ⌒

Take a deep breath, close your eyes and see yourself rightly, acknowledging that you are doing the best you can. As you grow and evolve, your field of receptivity becomes aligned to accept all the good you wish for.

CHAPTER 12

Master of Intention

The Time Is Now

LIFE IS A MAGNIFICENT ADVENTURE. You are the creator of your life, the orchestrator of your adventure. To become masterful in creating a life that is a masterpiece, it takes consistent bold intention. YOU now have the tools to begin living an intentional life and the key to becoming masterful at doing so. Your toolbox is full and ready for your journey.

At this time in human history, it is more important than ever to stay awake and conscious as you participate in this life experience. There is so much occurring in our world that is calling for our attention and intention. You being fully present as a conscious participant at this time on Earth is vital. Each one of us is important in the puzzle of life. Our challenges and our joys are only rich material to work with as we evolve and grow. Knowing we are not alone, we are connected energetically to one another, and we are supported by an unlimited Universal presence gives us the inner strength to carry onward.

The access point is you. Spiritual technology resides within your soul, and your willingness to keep your channel clear and available is the key to mastery. Listen to your inner knower, allow every breath to cleanse and prepare you for the unlimited wisdom to move through you.

ACTIVATE YOUR INTENTION TO MASTER LIVING A LIFE OF INTENTION

There is nowhere outside yourself you have to look. Lean into Spirit and allow your inner sanctuary to be lifted by your choice to stay conscious in what you create. Stay conscious and alert and remember to remember who you are, an unlimited being with precious and unique gifts. You came here to deliver your gifts!

You now have what you need, the tools to create consciously. Your toolbox is overflowing! As you amplify the daily practices offered within these pages, you will continue to fill your toolbox with a depth of wisdom that is palpable. It is a never-ending process as you continue to grow and evolve.

My intention is to master living a life of intention!

You will come to embody an automatic response system that is supported by your willingness to amplify the tools when needed. They are in place to lift you when challenges arise and guide you to see the light of Truth. Hold close to your heart the technology to live a life of intention. You have the key to stay out of expectation and boldly create intentions that support your dreams and desires.

You have the ability and the information, now I ask that you have a willingness to take your ability and information and keep it engaged and plugged into the Universe. I ask that you be willing to practice even when times are difficult. I ask that you be willing to grow your practice and continue to evolve. Practice, and as you master one tool, then begin with the next and then another and another. Become masterful applying the tools in your toolbox that will forevermore assist you to consciously create!

Choose to review the Three Power Pillars as you write your own power-packed intentions. The pillars will guide your words and your aim. They are the captain of your ship, the director of your precious and personal life experience. If you discover some hidden expectations, as quickly as you can, turn them around to strong intentions.

As you begin each day by intention, you will have the ability to observe choices before you, and as you decide which path to take, always ask yourself:

Does this choice honor my intention? Is it in alignment with what I am calling forth?

If the answer is no, then you have clarity and your decision will be guided by that clarity. Your actions must be in alignment with your intentions. If the answer is a resounding YES, this action is in alignment with the intention, then move forward into motion. When we practice the tool of this one question, we experience life with more ease and grace. This calls for pausing instead of reacting, and simply checking in with our soul agreement and the intention before us. Our actions must follow our intentions. Clarity is power, your intentions bring clarity. This determines your actions and in turn propels all you desire to you!

YOUR SPIRITUAL TOOLBOX IS READY!

Recently, while being interviewed, it was brought to my attention that in explaining the power of intention, it can be represented clearly as a bow and arrow. Think of the bow as the power of the Universe, solid, steady, consistent, firm and unlimited. The arrow is our intention. As we set our intention (the arrow) with positive clarity in the present moment and based on qualities, we can place it in the bow with confidence. The arrow is the energetic life force of our intentions and, as we aim and let go, our job is to surrender to the power of the bow and trust the Universe. The arrow does not concern itself with the how, the arrow trusts its nature and the sacred wisdom of the bow.

So, may we now trust ourselves to aim with high velocity for all our dreams and visions, and the dreams of the world to be made manifest. This is our charge, as our aim is important, our aim requires a practice that is lived; our aim requires a soul that is willing.

Stay open to learning and growing each and every day. Say yes to living as an eternal student. We are evolving beings and are here to continue to learn, expand and grow with every breath we take. What you know today will only be a glimmer of what you will know next year and the year after. Keep your heart open to allowing the technology of intention to be your springboard to all that is possible for you to create in this lifetime. Take the knowledge and live it so that you actively participate in this technological force. It is here for you, and your awakening is calling!

Knowledge is information; wisdom is what we do with that Information. Wisdom is living what we know!

This is our journey, to create from the platform of wisdom, to walk hand-in-hand with one another, activating every tool that we were given when we came into this life that we forgot about. You no longer have to forget. Your wake-up call has come!

As you now stand bow in hand, remove your arrow from its sheath, take a breath, set your intention with bold power, infuse it into the arrow, point it in the direction and let go.

TRULY, LET GO!

Now, practice what you know, step-by-step. Listen for inner guidance and take the actions that are in alignment with your desires.

My intention is to fully embody my spiritual technology and live a life of powerful intention!

Trust that you will know in which direction to move, for Spirit never leaves us and is always guiding us. Your power resides at your point of connection with this divine presence within you.

Stand in your knowing and be grateful. The Universe awaits your willingness to connect.

Be grateful you have an opportunity in this lifetime to live and amplify your wisdom and live your truth. You are tapping into the unlimited power of the Universe. The power is within you. Activate, celebrate and live the technology of intention!

❦ REMEMBER ❦

Take a breath, begin again.
With every breath we begin again.

www.ingramcontent.com/pod-product-compliance
Lightning Source LLC
Jackson TN
JSHW081316130125
77033JS00011B/313